THE FIRST PERSON SINGULAR

Northwestern University
Studies in Phenomenology
and
Existential Philosophy

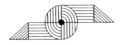

THE FIRST PERSON SINGULAR

Alphonso Lingis

Northwestern University Press
Evanston, Illinois

Northwestern University Press
www.nupress.northwestern.edu

Printed in the United States of America

10 9 8 7 6 5 4 3 2

ISBN-13: 978-0-8101-2412-7 (cloth)
ISBN-10: 0-8101-2412-2 (cloth)
ISBN-13: 978-0-8101-2413-4 (paper)
ISBN-10: 0-8101-2413-0 (paper)

Library of Congress Cataloging-in-Publication Data

Lingis, Alphonso, 1933–
    The first person singular / Alphonso Lingis.
        p. cm. — (Northwestern University studies in phenomenology and existential philosophy)
    Includes bibliographical references.
    ISBN-13: 978-0-8101-2412-7 (cloth : alk. paper)
    ISBN-10: 0-8101-2412-2 (cloth : alk. paper)
    ISBN-13: 978-0-8101-2413-4 (pbk. : alk. paper)
    ISBN-10: 0-8101-2413-0 (pbk. : alk. paper)
    1. Self (Philosophy) 2. Agent (Philosophy) 3. Subject (Philosophy)
I. Title. II. Series: Northwestern University studies in phenomenology & existential philosophy.
BD450.L5193 2007
126—dc22
                                                            2007006132

⊗ The paper used in this publication meets the minimum requirements of the American National Standard for Information Sciences—Permanence of Paper for Printed Library Materials, ANSI Z39.48-1992.

Contents

THE FIRST PERSON SINGULAR

Part 1

Being Here

1

A Chance to Be

A bacteria slipped into our porous bodies, multiplied. The infection spread. A virus—HIV, HTLV, Hantavirus, Marburg, Junin, Sabia, Machupo, Lassa, Oropuche virus, Ebola, Dengue, Rift Valley Fever—drifted in on a kiss and a love bite, on a sandwich we ate, a glass of water we drank, the air we breathed. Somewhere some cells of our bodies began twisting and feeding on our lifeblood, and one day a cancer metastasized. There are forty thousand fatal car crashes a year in the United States. "Die at the right time!" Friedrich Nietzsche enjoined,[1] thinking of great leaders who outlasted their victories and lived on, bored and indifferent to administration, which their obsequious subordinates corrupted; thinking too of gifted and brave men and women who were cut down before their work was accomplished. But death comes when it will. From the outside, an accident, death cuts short the will in our life to extend time for itself.

But is not our life too an accident? Out of millions of spermatozoa repeatedly ejected into a vagina, this one, thrashing blindly, caught hold of an ovum and it swelled and divided. One day I was born. The causes that are responsible for the particularity of my body lie in the confluence of genetic, biochemical, and environmental forces at the moment that I was conceived and during the course of my embryonic development. With the slightest alteration of any strand of this network of forces there would instead be nothing, or there would have been conceived in that womb someone who, however similar to me, would not be me at all.

Physicists, chemists, biologists, and geneticists provide determinist explanations for what look like strokes of good or bad luck. The more that I study their findings, the less I can see my existence anywhere programmed in the electromagnetic fields, the molecular attractions and collisions, and the meanderings of evolution. Beneath me, behind me, there is nothing that demanded me, required this I.

See nature setting out by day the intricate designs of alpine flowers, flashing the crystal colors of the 319 species of hummingbirds. See the night lofting the powdery wings of 10,500 species of moths in North America, uncoiling huge flowers in the tropics. See the tiny rainbows flashing briefly on bubbles in the surf and the streaming vermilions and indigos of 25,000 species of coral fish. See how the setting sun emblazons the skies with unnamable colors different every evening, different every minute of the evening.

It is also by chance that the earth has glaciers, sequoias, giraffes, quetzals, chameleons, and orchids.

The sense of being separate and on our own is precarious. We are haunted by the possibility that our sense that we are conducting our lives is illusory. The possibility that our autonomy is abusive and pernicious makes us doubt its justification and validity.

2

How I Come to Be Here

How do *I* come to be here? How does a conscious individual arise in the material world, in a living organism?

We awaken and, finding ourselves supported, stir and move, our movements assured of the continuing support of the ground. We find ourselves immersed in light and darkness; air; warmth and cold; and in the density of colors, tones, and textures.[1] Awakened sensibility maintains contact with this boundless reality. This sensibility is not recording a multiplicity of sense-data; it is the reassuring sense of the ground that extends indefinitely beneath and ahead; the pleasurable sense of the continuity of light and darkness, air and warmth; the quickening sense of finding ourselves in lustrous and reverberant expanses. In enjoying the support and sustenance of the elements, sensibility intensifies into a sense of me being here. I feel myself in buoyant, fluid, or throbbing pleasure, in equanimity, composure, or apathy; and in boredom, melancholy, or anxiety. The I is an *I enjoy, I endure, I suffer.*

A living organism is a material composition that holds itself together circulating fluids and distributing nutrients according its circadian rhythms. It excretes waste products and it is porous: substance leaks, evaporates from it, heat escapes. Lacks, determined by the composition it seeks to maintain, develop. An inner awareness turns these lacks into needs and wants, into hunger, thirst, cold, and fatigue. These open the organism to the outside environment, awakening the perception and action that seek substances to satisfy its needs.[2] When these contents are assimilated—the liquid has been absorbed, the food consumed—an inner awareness in the form of contentment simmers over them. The sense of oneself is an *I need, I want, I am contented.*

Our bodies see and hear by moving among things and manipulating them.[3] In the shapes and colors of things and in their density, elasticity, or fluidity, they perceive forces. In the sheen of the knife they see its hardness and sharpness; in the shuddering patches of dull light in the mud they see gummy suction; in the continuous dense gray of the concrete they perceive the solid support of the sidewalk down which we advance. Our eyes and hands catch on to a real or possible relationship between the force in a material thing and what that force can loosen, separate, or set into motion. I find myself in perceiving paths ahead that support my advance and a layout of things that yield to or resist my forces. I am where my bodily and affective forces are integrated, manipulate things, and confront obstacles. The sense of oneself that arises in a body in action is an *I can*. How our bodies are affected by outside forces reverberates as feelings of delight, fascination, repugnance, or boredom; how attention is focused and energies channeled on things reverberates as emotions of excitement, buoyancy, thrill, relief, or lassitude.

The force in things that we can use to loosen, separate, or set into motion other things also exists in those other things; every objective is a possible implement in turn. Every practical initiative engages further practical initiatives. Practical activity is not terminated by the satisfaction of needs.

The practical layout of paths, implements, objectives, and obstacles is staked out in the elemental depths with which sensibility maintains contact and tends to sink back into them. The laborer climbs the ladder to the roof, surveys the layout of the rafters and sheathing boards. Soon the hand grasping and wielding the hammer, positioning and pounding in the nail, shifts from an initiative into a rhythm that goes on by itself. The roof shifts from a viewed structure into the solidity of a support being felt. The purposive attention fades out, leaving an unfocused sensibility that enjoys the vibrancy of the rhythm of hammering in the radiance of the skies and the freshness of the breeze.

A living organism gets hungry and thirsty as it needs to refurbish substances and energies used to maintain itself. But a kitten or an otter gets hungry and thirsty after spending so much of its energies in play. A human brain uses some 20 percent of the body's energy, nutrients, and oxygen, but most of our mental activity is not engaged in problem solving of biological needs; our brain is largely employed in paying attention to everybody else's business and in improvising streams of amusing nonsense with our coworkers and friends, in processing the unendingly varied vast landscapes we view as we go for a drive in the country or processing the fast-paced television dramas in the evening. A living organism generates energies in excess of what it requires to launch the movements to satisfy its needs.

Superabundant energies make one feel good to be healthy, to be alive; the mind dreams, creates visions of what is not there; the body dances, moves without going anywhere. In the exhilaration produced by superabundant health and strength and boundless mental curiosity arises an exultant I, dancing across the fields of needs and implements.

* * *

Conscious life is not a steady state; it moves from the eclipse of consciousness in sleep to the tasks and pleasures of our everyday environment. The rhythms of life are interrupted by *experiences.* The term "experience" has come in philosophy to designate any conscious state, but in ordinary language "having an experience" designates a time when we are surprised by sudden and unexpected encounters with something or someone and abruptly find ourselves in an impassioned state. Experiences are marked by astonishment, outbursts of joy, fear, anger, and woe.

Impassioned encounters are lived in high intensity and with quickened and amassed energies. They begin in surprise; they are commencements. Anger erupts with maximum heat and intensity right away; shame occurs at once. Fear breaks out over what we sense is just about to happen.

Impassioned energies bring out into high relief and closeness the enigmatic, disquieting, enthralling, or threatening character of something or someone suddenly before us. Wonder circumscribes an event or layout, as the background of the familiar and predictable fades away. Anger demarcates the front lines of the unacceptable, intolerable, the contours of an injustice. Erotic excitement zooms in on a charged carnal shape and substance in the midst of functionally clothed men, women, and children whom we pass on the sidewalk.

In wonder, fear, or grief, the broad field of our plans, deliberations, and rememberings abruptly fades out. Sudden astonishment, rage, cupidity, or anguish occupies the whole of consciousness. Anger overwhelms and drives out fear; the grip of fear drives out anger and mourning. A passion fills up the present; it does not divide its energies so as to maintain past attitudes or consider consequences. The shock and agitations of bewilderment, the release of breath gasping "Ah!" in wonder, the collapse and tears of grief, the trembling and nausea of fear are not signals I produce for witnesses. Passions are nonironic.

We sense inwardly and immediately the difference between anger, mourning, guilt, and shame, and between hope, fear, greed, despair, and courage. They have different objects and distinctive tensions and tonalities. Although we have witnessed acts of courage and imagined what we would do in dangerous situations, only when we find ourselves faced with violent aggressors or in a situation where others are trapped in a burning building, and act, will we understand what courage is. We do not really know jealousy until we find ourselves in its grip. The paranoid being on the lookout for dangers and threats does not make us know fear; instead it works to warily avoid situations where fear may arise.

Although we say that fury or jealously "came over me," that "I don't know what happened to me," in reality our sense of ourselves is most concentrated and intense in these experiences. I am not at a distance from my trembling, recoiling, tightening body, my blushes, my sobbing; I am completely in my rage, my jealousy, my astonishment.

In impassioned states I find myself to be on my own. Before an imminent threat, terror outlines the boundaries and contours of my life. Though others also may be mourning the child, lover, or friend I have lost, my grief is mine, and I cannot detach myself from it. Jealousy, obsessed with others suffocatingly close to me, disconnects me from the everyday layout of common concerns. In anger the life I find beset by injustice, by injury or insult, is my own. The I, singularized and brought to a peak of concentration and intensity, is *I am thrilled, I am delighted, I am enraged, I am terrified.*

In ancient and classical literature, passions gave individuals their identity. In Homer, the Greek tragedies, medieval epics, Renaissance chronicles and theories of political power, and Elizabethan theater, the outbursts, collisions, and abrupt reversals of passions define the actions and destinies of individuals and the conflicts and crises in societies.

The philosophy of mind, however, put aside the different states that we have noted in which a specific sense of oneself arises, to envision something selfsame and abiding designated by the word "I." Modern philosophy rejected knowledge of substances as metaphysical and in particular rejected the religious-metaphysical notion of the soul as an abiding substance. The individual ego would instead be the sum total of states and acts of perception and will, integrated into associative or significant patterns, available to memory. This self is essentially private; what others can see of me in any given situation or range of situations is not equivalent to the unity of the self constituting itself in remembrance.

The theory of the ego did not start with impassioned states, when a sense of oneself is at a peak of concentration and intensity. The very word "passions" was replaced with a vocabulary of "emotions," "feelings," "sentiments," and "moods."[1] These terms are conceived as designating intermittent attributes or drives. The ego is something apart from them; it can consider them, distance itself from them, humor them, and maintain an ironic stance with regard to them.

Fundamental to modern psychology is the notion of the ambivalence of emotions: we can both love our parents and resent them in our longing to be independent; we can feel both triumphant and guilty for having put someone down; we can both grieve for the infant we have aborted and feel relief over our new freedom. The ambivalence of feelings and emotions justifies the possibility and need for supervision and control of them.

The modern conception of the ego and its emotions, feelings, sentiments, and moods is congruent with the concern, in modern mercantile society, to maintain continuity and regularity in our perceived and practicable environment and to measure our drives and forces to the scale and proportion of practical tasks at hand. Practical concerns favor long-view considerations and calculation of our interests and the elimination of disruptive impassioned states. In reality, however, modern mercantile society endorses avarice, the passion that excludes the disruptive short-term passions of anger, grief, falling in love, as well as shame, regret, and mourning.[5]

Impassioned states, seen as disruptions of the integrated and socialized individual and of the effective operation of mercantile society, have been marginalized and pathologized in the philosophy of mind. But they remain central in literature and drama viewed in theater, cinema, or television, as well as in the depictions of social and political conflicts, economic enterprises, and market trends diffused in the media, where we also find understanding of our lives.

3

Where I Am

Mapping the Environment

In the boundless expanses of light, air, and warmth where luminous and resounding substances extend over the supporting ground, we establish a site from which we depart and to which we return. Our home base is not simply a shelter for a collection of implements; it is a zone of intimacy and tranquillity.[1] It is closed off from the bustle of the workplaces and markets. Its furnishings—the armchair, the seats on the balcony—merge with the substance of our body to which they give support and rest. The hi-fi and the TV fill a space with entertainment separated from practical concerns; the plants, the fish tank, the back garden welcome sustaining nature.

When we were just driving across the state, this town was a flux of visual patterns passing across the car window. Now, we have arrived to live here. We take a room in a hotel or rent a house. Then we lay out a Main Street that extends from our door to our place of work, and side streets leading to the grocery store, the laundry, the bank and post office, the cinema and the bars. We establish pathways, envision objectives, take hold of implements and encounter obstacles.

Things that are used are first grasped and taken possession of: they are substances closed in themselves.[2] Things are means, but they are also ends; they satisfy our hungers and respond to our needs, and they attract our sensibility and sensuality. They are annexed to the zone of tranquillity and intimacy, kept on hand for enjoyment.

The area we map out with practical intentions and objectives is limited. The work spaces of the carpenter or of the nurse making rounds in the hospital by night do not extend instrumental relations unendingly across the world.[3] The grocery, the laundry, and our workplace in the factory, office, or hospital are zones we stake out with practical initiatives, but they are also places of relaxation and shared pleasure. For us to live here is to have a home here, to enjoy this town, these forests at the edge of the ocean or these rice-terraced mountains, these northern or tropical skies.

What lies beyond the paths and implements we use and the objectives we work toward is not only the background of what is just on hand, what has broken down, been used up, is in the way, or has been left aside:[4] beyond lies the alien, the elemental. Beyond are earth, light, air, and skies, elements not enclosed within surfaces, extending indefinitely in the distances and in depth.

Rhythmic and Melodic Space

A living organism is a material composite in which blood, nutrients, and energies circulate according to multiple circadian periodicities. Its sensory organs pick up vibratory stimuli at their thresholds that vary with levels in the biochemical homeostasis of the body. Its sensitive surfaces record movement, rumble, pressure, texture, and substance with quiverings, tinglings, pacings, and strokings.

We shift position, relax, tense up, assume one posture and then another, advance and retreat, avoid things, manipulate things. We shudder, rock, sway, swing, pump, prance, and gesticulate. Surges of superabundant energy become vibrant and intensify in exhilaration, then subside. We advance into the outside environment and act, then return to our home base. Particular initiatives are generalized and become habitual. The behaviors of our body cannot be explained as reactions to the impact of physical stimuli, but they also are not a succession of initiatives launched each time in view of objectives. There is a rhythmic and melodic structure to body movements.

The rhythm of our breath is internally coded, but it takes on the pulse of the atmosphere weighted with humidity in tropical lowlands or of the jittery wind in the air thinned out at high altitudes. Our heartbeat synchronizes with the onrush of exciting or menacing events and, at night, with the ticktock of the clock. Our circadian rhythms pace our inner organs with the cycle of day and night and with the lunar month and the seasons. When we walk, we set up a certain gait according to the intensity of our energy or our languor, but our stride or amble takes up the rhythm of the rocky or sandy ground and that of the waves against the beach. It catches on to the pace of a companion.

What the neuropsychologist Alexander Romanovich Luria named "kinetic melodies"[5] and which Gilles Deleuze and Félix Guattari call "refrains"[6] establish our home base, extend practicable zones about it, and open lines of departure into the outlying world.

An infant not yet able to move about and handle things, or a child in the dark feeling adrift, reassures herself in humming. Her humming, taking up the movements and vibrancy of the air, sets up a center in the dark or drifting space. A lullaby localizes the baby's slumber for her. Rustling the bedcovers or the papers on the desk, sighing and coughing, humming or whistling, the child or the adult maintains a *here* present and maintains his or her presence here. We rock our feet while sitting, finger our hair, hum or whistle, and pump our hands while walking in the flow of the landscape.

The morning ritual—ablutions, breakfast, the newspaper—is not a succession of deliberated initiatives. Our home base is not set before us as a spectacle; it is a rhythm of rooms passing, each with its own chromatic tone and hue and intensity of light. Our clothing, furnishings, kitchen nooks and dining rooms, and the plants, windows, and gardens form rhythmic patterns; we respond to them—making the bed, washing the dishes, and relaxing in the back garden—with kinetic refrains. We move back and forth with the staccato of the morning light or the continuo of its afternoon gloom.

We leave for work. The tree-sheltered houses bob up and down as we bicycle by them; we join in the pace and beat of the crowds pressing up and down the sidewalk during rush hour. Opening the window, parking our coat and lunch, and laying out our tools mark out our work space for us. The professional greetings and responses of office workers, as the cries of woodcutters, the work songs of Volga boatmen, make work a job that we have somewhere. With his cries the street vendor marks out the space where he distributes snacks or garments, the Muzak in shopping malls locates in the din and rumble of the city the area where workers pile up mass-produced commodities to its rhythms and clerks ring up sales.

Appropriate and effective movements arise where the body's inner "music of the muscles"[7] picks up the sonorous or silent refrains outside. They respond to the patterns and recurrences in the layout of things, move with the rhythms of fellow-workers or shoppers and the beat or murmur of space, in the advancing light of the day and dark of the night, and in the turning of the seasons. The rhythms and kinetic melodies give rise to a sense of what the neurologist Oliver Sacks called the "active and free I": active in that the inner forces of the body maintain its internal organization, circulating its nutrients, generating energies, and releasing its superabundant energies; free in that its perceptions and movements are not simple reactions to the impact of outside forces nor driven by the urgencies of need and want.[8] When we feel we are being forced to do things not at our own rate, we feel alienated from ourselves.

Our departures are not simply launched with willful intentions; they catch on to refrains echoing in the distances. A woman opens the door to call someone or let someone in. With a stride and a good-bye and a "Hi there!" she sets forth, swinging her arms or swaying her hips, power walking or clacking her heels, making her own way through shortcut or detour to the town and to the hills.

With a shift of pace we acknowledge the office we return to after a lunch hour stroll window-shopping, the mountain we have reached after a long amble across the fields. The Australian Aborigines note the rhythms and melodies of the landscape and make their way across the continent by following its songlines.

Hearing distant melodies, we can set forth from the zone we inhabit, never to return. Salmon at breeding season leave the territories where they live and return to where they were born to lay their eggs and die. Periodically the lobsters of the Caribbean march off in single file into the open ocean; biologists believe that their long march follows the advance of glacial periods on Earth, the last one ten thousand years ago. Migratory birds, responding to the seasonal tilting of Earth in its orbit, follow the lines of Earth's magnetic field. Twelve thousand years ago, small bands of humans made their way across the uncharted glaciers into the American hemisphere as the blizzards effaced their paths. Mountain climbers and explorers of uninhabitable regions, jungle, desert, or the ice continent seek to approach the abysses of death. To the lure of marching bands, men and women go off to the cacophony of foreign wars, not bothering to make the politician's objectives and reasons their own, go off to die. Sadhus in India, as also pilgrims in medieval Europe, leave their homes in search of inhuman and superterrestrial realms.

Impassioned Spaces

Passions grasp at once the astonishing, enthralling, or terrifying cast of an event or situation that is suddenly before us and disconnect it from the outlying field of continuities and regularities that occupy everyday concerns. They fix attention and set in motion a restlessness of the eyes, which pass back and forth from the focal object to the background and jump from one feature to the next. Our *experiences* are not intermittent events that happen to us in the world—the common world, the world of nature, the everyday world—and that impassioned responses simply bring into focus. In astonishment, anger, jealousy, and lust we find ourselves in a space that is our own.

Anger and indignation mark out the contours of the intolerable, the unacceptable, the unjust, as does forgiveness. They bring out the zone where I, and those I care for and care about, live and act and must not be encroached upon. Joy and magnanimity, and also ambition and greed, expand my vital space toward luminous horizons others do not see. Terror shrinks space, which closes in on me.

. The space of a passion has its distinctive internal structure. Passions mark out gradations of closeness to and remoteness from me. (Aristotle notes that when we feel fear for someone, abruptly that someone appears bound to us in closeness or intimacy; when we feel pity for someone, that someone appears separate and distant from us.)[9] In terror we see an initial cause quickly cascading into evil utterly disproportionate in severity and finality.[10] With outbursts of laughter we see a sequence of breakdowns in causality end up with an outcome that is trivial or harmless. Mourning effaces the relief of space, making directions appear equivalent and empty.

Impassioned experiences, which erupt, endure, and come to an end, contain a vivid sense of time—of a stretch of personal time cut off from the public or common time as from the time of nature. The time of anger or shame is that of the immediate past still flanking the present. This immediate past is my own past, while the events of the social world and of nature recede into the common and anonymous past. It is disconnected from the expanse of the past phases of our life with which we are intermittently in touch through recall, with which we lose contact through forgetfulness. It is not that expanse of the past but my immediate past revealed in anger or shame that excludes fear or hope.

The imminent future we face in fear or hope is cut off from the field of possibilities and eventualities with which we are in touch through intermittent acts of calculation, planning, and reasoned decision. The imminent future is a different zone or medium of time, not simply the continuation of the world's presence, the universal and anonymous time of the continual oncoming of things and events.

The time of each impassioned experience has its own rate and pace. The time of a terrifying experience is dilated in the pounding of our heart and transfixed in our eyes that see the collision or the fall in slow motion. In fascination, time extends without our having a sense of how much or how little. In wonder, the internal differentiation of time dissolves and duration becomes something like eternity, an immobile present. In frantic desperation, time sprints ahead.

Passions erupt, reach a pitch, and endure for a time proper to each, fading off in exhaustion. The anger over an insult, injury, or aggression arises at once and strikes at once. A response that has been delayed too long is no longer driven by anger: it has become deliberate, fed by imagination, and strikes someone who is no longer engaged in the act that provoked wrath, who is no longer the same person. Mourning that has ended too quickly shows others—and ourselves—that it was but the per-functory gestures of mourning; mourning that goes on too long is acedia, despondency, depression, or obsessive fixation.[11]

Impassioned experiences are states of high energy and issue in agitations and actions. Anger works itself out in revenge, fear in flight. The time of mourning is a time in which we need to work out what we have lost in losing a friend, parent, or lover and learn how to live with his or her memory and persistent presence in our thoughts and actions.

An impassioned state can maintain its intensity but abruptly convert from jealousy to rage, from wrath to mourning or shame, from ambition to guilt. Typically these conversions are one-way only: rage does not convert into jealousy, love or guilt into ambition. If jealousy does follow rage, or ambition follow guilt or love, it is because the first state has faded away or been interrupted and the new passion provoked by some encounter or mishap. Many impassioned states are abruptly transformed into embarrassment or shame when we encounter another impassioned person or when the operations of the social world impose themselves on us.

An impassioned state can end with a decisive act in which all the energies and the tonality of the passion are discharged. Most murders that are not done in gang wars are "crimes of passion": an individual, tormented by jealousy, humiliated, enraged, kills a lover, spouse, ex-spouse, rival, even his or her child or the child of a rival lover. The deed is to the full measure of the rage, humiliation, jealousy, whose vehemence is often forthwith converted into guilt, self-loathing, or pure love of the victim.

Often several divergent or conflicting passions are aroused by a rapid succession of events or by the same object or event showing different aspects at different times or in different perspectives. A lover who is tender and affectionate and then petulant and judgmental arouses love and devotion and also frustration and anger. We can find ourselves worn down, exhausted by the clash of vehement responses in us; we withdraw from the object of our passionate involvement, seek to regard it from a distance, to achieve what we call "objectivity" about it. We judge what we see of our lover in different situations as subordinate aspects of a whole, his or her nature, which we envision through a unifying concept.[12]

Marking Our Space

Coral fish mark their territories by displaying their ostentatious colors and patterns; birds parade their flamboyant plumage, and their songs make their territories resonate for them. Changing into white collar and gray flannel, a student or blue-collar worker takes over a new place in the industrial or commercial zone. By acquiring the "in" garb and body decoration, a young woman newly arrived in the city claims a circuit of clubs as her territory. With his tattoos, a longshoreman marks a section of the waterfront as his domain, or a biker claims as his the open roads where the Hell's Amish ride.[13]

Adjusting their posture and gait, mobilizing their forces to manipulate resources and circumvent obstacles, our bodies respond to what is in the environment. With expressive movements—outcries, posturings, displays, and gestures and rituals—we stake out and mark our space. Such expressions do not exteriorize concepts and intentions first formed in our minds. They couple onto things and situations, circumscribe and segment them, and slow down movements or accelerate them. They detach our bodies from things and events or expose them to more distant things and events.

After her ascent up the narrow ladder, a diver's two steps on the diving board anticipate the free space of the dive. Looking out into the empty space and with a nod of his head, a hang glider, now balanced, launches his run and takeoff from the cliff. With its pirouette before an outbreak of good luck, our body disconnects from the dull imperatives of everyday necessities. As a reader reads, her fingers drum on the table, her feet do a two-step under it, her fingers gyrate in the streaming strands of her hair—dances with which, as her attention turns into the space of the novel, her body disconnects from the ordered layout of the public library.

A smile, a shout, a handshake, an embrace, or laughter circumscribe or break open a sector of space. The hand that hails a friend seen at a distance short-circuits across the path and all the intervening things to make contact. With lifted arms and nods we affirm the initiative our spokesperson is launching, pledging our allegiance to the speaker and to the action: "Right on!" Responding to someone's reproaches with an abrupt show of the upturned third finger, we close off the demand for an explanation and a justification. Fights too are expressive. An argument gets settled with a fight—especially an argument about our courage, our honor, our loyalty, or the sincerity and strength of our conviction. With the fight we clear the space for ourselves or are closed off from it.

There are spaces in which we cannot envision or formulate objectives or grasp onto anything usable but which we embrace with a tender, incredulous, or awestruck gaze. Nothing meaningful we can say can connect with his suffering, but our hand reaches out to stroke the arm of the dying stranger.

An unknown person left a gym bag in a gay pub in Soho; after he left, the homemade nail bomb in it exploded, killing three people and slashing the flesh and eyes of a hundred others. The next day at the police barricade people placed flowers. All day and all evening people were coming to visit the site, contemplating the growing pile of bouquets. They were marking the place of the aggression against gay people and other marginals as their own. They walked away silently; there was nothing to say.

In Peter Weir's film *The Last Wave,* the lawyer who is defending some urban Aborigines who have killed another Aborigine for, they say, having violated tribal law, goes to search out a tribal elder who seems to have a hold on them. He finds an old man seated on the floor of an empty room. "Who are you?" the lawyer asks. The old man answers, "Who are you?" repeating the question in diminuendo, "who are you . . . who are you . . . who are you . . . who are you . . . ," his voice finally shifting into humming. The humming begins to reverberate about this white lawyer the songlines with which Aboriginal Australia has been mapped out since the dreamtime. The lawyer leaves, without having heard words he could appropriate and explicate in the offices and courts.

Expressions segment and punctuate situations and events and themselves come to an end. We do not generalize the ritual of piling flowers at the sites of urban aggressions. We sense that expressions lose their force when repeated in more diverse and ever-wider contexts, where interpretation begins and will be required. As words interpret an expression, we sense the disconnection in the abstraction that makes words repeatable and in words whose functioning nowise changes when what they name or designate is no longer there. When someone dies, Australian Aborigines cease pronouncing the name with which the person was hailed and addressed, and if the person had done paintings, museum curators of collections of Aboriginal art will have to remove paintings bearing that name from public display.

Part 2

The Voice

4

The Voice That Makes Contact

Murmuring Spaces

We woke up one Saturday and turned on the radio; our apartment was filled with the voice of the usual newscaster, a faceless voice that we don't have to pay attention to or answer. We showered, boiled water for coffee, and fried eggs. Outside, the trills and calls of birds glittered in the dry autumn leaves of the trees. We decided to skip our aerobics hour in the gym and take a long walk instead. We felt we had gotten out of the town when the muttering of the sparse Saturday morning traffic faded away in the thin hum of insects in the fields and the whir of the breeze. From time to time a steady rumble of a car approaching extended the road behind and ahead of us. Some time later the roar of planes arriving or departing spread out the airport zone ahead. Then, entering the woods, the rustling of leaves and the occasional thrashing of squirrels rose about us. From the bottom came the gurgling of the stream lurching over rocks. Once outside the woods, the yapping, howling, or growling of various kinds of dogs segmented our way through a neighborhood of small houses on big lots. Finally among the hubbub of traffic the greetings and laughter of students hanging out made us aware we had come to the town of Saturday evening.

During our walk, the ambient sonority extended space and differentiated zones and distances. The differing spaces were not exposed and measured by sight. Here and there something drew our attention—an objective hung at the end of the look. Sometimes our eyes held this objective in focus as we approached it. The rest of the time our eyes were not scanning the space for something to look at; they were lulled by the rhythms of the roadside growth of crown vetch and goldenrod. Our gaze drifted in the flow of the fields and of the clouds over them, in the play of light on the stream and its mossy banks, without measuring their breadth or depth.

Consonance and Dissonance

Our voice does not produce sound out of silence. It resounds with the tone and density of the wind coursing through the body's tubes and bellows, shaping melodies and words in the ambient air that is traversed with so many whispers and calls. It joins the drone and crackle and outbursts of things and the murmur of the environment.

In greeting someone with "Hey man!" the cocky tone of those words hail in that individual the man, not a student, a waiter, or a stranger. We catch on to the urgent, anxious, jumpy, elated, or flabbergasted tone of someone who addresses us; her voice resounds in our response. To answer the frenetic tone of a young person who bursts into our office with the stentorian tone of settled and regulated officious life is, before we refuse to understand really what she will tell us, to refuse her tone—to refuse her.

We catch on to the purring of the kitten, the piping of the spring frogs, the desolate cries of the lost duckling, the keening of the orphaned monkey. We pick up the tone of the fishing village at the edge of the tropical island, the flowering dunes of the desert, the glaciers of the Andes. As our words form, the tone of these things and events resounds in our voice. The pacing and accents of our phrases express the calm or the frenetic movement, the rhythm and periodicity or jerks and explosions of the things and events. Our words articulate the agitated tone of a column of ants, the syncopation of the dockworkers unloading a ship, the purple majesty of the Pacific Ocean under dawning Madagascar skies. Our words reverberate the tone of a dance, a cave, a cathedral—the pacing, the rhythms, the expanse; they return the muffled or dead silence.

While walking with a friend to see the forest, we speak of what is around us. Our words are movements that greet trees, rocks, or forest denizens standing or moving there; summon forth things discreetly withdrawn into the forest population; bring out or emphasize shapes and behaviors; only note what needs to have been said but once; slide over things; and leave reserved or shy things in silence. The general or particularizing words, the predications and qualifying adverbs, and the grammatical construction of phrases do not diagram the ways things are laid out in the forest. Yet a language filling the rustle and hum of nature with commonplace identifications and sentimental clichés or with frivolous, platitudinous, or abstract talk about the forest separates from the forest visible and audible about us. What we say is interspersed with rejections of inappropriate ways of speaking and categorizing: "No, it's not that . . ."

Our remarks, exclamations, and ruminations respond and correspond—in their tone, pacing, and precision of wording—to the way light and shadow, colors, shapes, and horizons take form, are drawn out, break up, intensify, move andante or with staccato outbursts with the pacing of our walk and the sweep of our gaze. Our words do not simply depict the forest that is visible; they actively explore and reveal;[1] they slow down and intensify the contact our bodies are making with things and events or accelerate them, turn them in new directions, focus the eyes and the hearing or let them drift. And the forest for its part thrusts events and shifts vistas before us that arouse questions and exclamations and reanimate our commentary.

As we soften our voices in the summer twilight, we listen in to the thin counterpoints of the reedy insect voices. In the restaurant buzzing with so many kinds of conversations, we vary the pitch and tones—indignant, solemn, giddy, or smug—of what we are saying to our friend. Our words do not march close, one upon another; we stammer, we leave silences that are just blanks and not meaningful silences, we daub in "uh"s and "mmm"s that are not placeholders for words we are searching for, we put in stock phrases and clichés that do not mean to draw in received truths but instead to lighten the seriousness of the conversation, take from it some or most of the weight of its meaningfulness or turn it into mere chatter. Quoting voices or repeating things we have just said, we raise or lower the pitch, repeat them in a flat or singsong manner, echo them in a lithe melody or a whisper, draw out the vowels and slam or hiss the consonants. Our voice is a wave rising and being moved across the rumbling and rustling, pounding and chattering earth and city. It relays and responds to the voices of things.

5

The Exploratory Voice

With motor and vocal refrains, and with words too, we stake out the territory. "Here, I see . . ." "Did you hear that report on the news yesterday that war is possible?" "Let's get back to the point." Such phrases establish a home base. We situate ourselves in our experience as an auto mechanic that stretches back fifteen years. We station ourselves within the present state of veterinary science and practice. We establish ourselves in texts of Freud or of Heidegger.

The angry voice demarcates the contours of the intolerable, of injustice. The fearful voice searches for refuges, marks directions of retreat and paths of flight. The voice in mourning marks out the contours and dimensions of the loss. When we speak about what we are doing or planning, our words bring out specific features of the situation and the implements and connect proximate with remote events; they may map out one situation upon another.

The exploratory advance is interrupted by exclamations, exhalations, hesitations, and silences. Statements, questions, hypotheses, and objections introduce new or different lines in the relief map. The movement of a discourse splits into radiating lines, returns upon itself, and comes to a stop at dead ends or conclusions. There are moments of closure, when several strands are braided together into integrated wholes and into generalizations.

The explanations of a mechanics manual lay out the order of assembly of a mechanism, show how a motorcycle works, and explain the causes of and solutions to breakdowns. Sociology and anthropology monographs diagram the kinship relations of a society and the division of labor based on them, portray the distribution and marketing of its resources, explicate its juridical and political systems, its cosmological or religious representations. Then they seek to map out the dynamics of these superimposed systems: how they work, how they intersect, how they endure. They may well draw on the stages of individual emotional and intellectual evolution depicted in psychology monographs to explain the economic productivity and political demands of a society whose population has a very high birth rate or which is rapidly aging.

Narratives map out sections of time. They explain events by showing the emergence of an event out of prior relevant circumstances and events.[1] Relevance and importance are specified differently in history, sociology, anthropology, aesthetics, and psychoanalysis. Subsequent events are invoked to identify present events as important, but these subsequent events invoked may not come to pass. The significance of discoveries, innovations, conflicts, victories, and defeats may well be explained differently by contemporary and by subsequent historians.

An empirical science is not simply an additive accumulation of observation reports; it is an explanatory system. The observation reports are sorted according to similarity, and more general statements, the laws of nature, are developed from them. The laws of nature explain the observation reports; they give rise to predictions: they are formulated such that, given the law, the observation reports can be deductively derived from it. The laws of nature can be coordinated in the construction of a theory. The theory explains the laws; it is formulated such that the laws can be deductively derived from it. The empirical laws and the theories map out zones in which the observed entities and events are located and are observed to—and predicted to—interact.

Any sufficiently extensive set of observation statements can give rise to more than one formulation of law and consequently more than one formulation of the theory.[2] The proliferation of laws and theories will be controlled by judgments that decide which formulations cover the most important cases, which serve best the coherence and simplicity of the discipline, and which function to suggest new domains and methods for empirical investigation.

We transport terms, relationships, models, and methods of organization from one field to another, to see what effects they would produce—if we introduced some of the language of psychoanalysis into political economy, some of the language of microbiology into psychoanalysis. When we carry some of the concepts and models from computer science over into cognitive science, we are not just reformulating the same phenomena in a different vocabulary; details and events that were not seen and articulated get identified and structured, things get related in new ways, some of the old paradigms are pushed out of the way. There are also languages that are inappropriate, whose discriminations are not at the right level, that make connections that oversimplify or that neglect relationships established in other disciplines—limiting the worth of the psychology of emotions introduced into musicology, the language of physical dynamics in economics, evolutionary biology in cultural anthropology.

6

Words That Organize and That Command

Words order our action: they organize our environment by segmenting it and demarcating paths and instrumental connections and by invoking possibilities and predicting consequences. They signal what has to be safeguarded, nurtured, repaired, or built, and they sort out resources and urgencies. Our words are not only indicative or informative but also imperative: they launch and command our action or inaction.

Numbers disconnected from anything but one another—1, 2, 100, 1,000, 1,000,000—can function as an organizing method. Numbers are the preeminent means of military organization for aggressive wars of indefinite expansion, for example, those of the great khans who thundered across the steppes of central Asia over the centuries.[1] Levying ten men from each village, a hundred from each town or each clan, constitutes an army. To each company a hundred horses are requisitioned; each town along the march is required to furnish ten beef cattle, a hundred measures of wheat and barley. The army will march across the steppe twenty miles each day. Five hundred cavalrymen will be sent to the east of the enemy camp, five hundred to the west. At the end of a raid or battle, losses will be expressed in numbers: we lost a hundred; the enemy lost five hundred.

Numbering and arithmetic organize multinational corporations whose production is diversified and whose assembly plants are located where labor and transportation costs are cheapest. They can organize individuals who determine what to major in in college on the basis of accessibility and salaries of various occupations, what percentage of their salaries to spend on the purchase of a house, what percentage for the education of their children, how many children to have, when to retire, and where to spend the rest of their days.

Part 3

Word of Honor

7

The Important and the Urgent

As we become intimate with persons, other animals, ecological systems, buildings, or artworks, we develop perceptual and conceptual sensitivity, logical acumen, breadth and depth of comprehension, and the capacity to distinguish the important from the trivial. Understanding is all that.

"Importance" is one of those words that are clearer than any set of words suggested to paraphrase it or from which it could be deduced. Other such words are "grand," "noble," "magnificent," "sublime," and "transcendent" in the Spanish sense.

"Importance" is not simply a term in a code or an abstract category. Everyone who acquired the concept of importance acquired it from experience with some human or other animal, ecological system, building, or artwork. Importance is seen in the baobab, in the Borobudur stupa, in the condor soaring over the glaciers of the Andes, in the fervor and incorruptibility of Steve Biko. To see them with perceptual and conceptual sensitivity, logical acumen, and breadth and depth of comprehension is to see their importance. The recognition of their importance does not derive from any justificatory procedure. It does not derive from generic statements about the importance of human life or the importance of forests for the chemical composition of the atmosphere.

Importance does not simply mean important to the speaker or user. To obtain a certain stamp may well be important to a stamp collector, but even he will not claim it is important, important purely and simply.[1] Importance does not mean important to outside reality—as though the Louvre, the human species, or planet Earth were important to the universe.

We distinguish between what is important for me—or for an industry, an institution, a culture, or an ecosystem—from what is simply important, that whose importance is intrinsic, perceived in it. It is important that Beethoven's *Missa Solemnis* be rehearsed to perfection. An unnoticed act of honesty by a woman in an old folks' home is important.

There is grandeur in the size of the pyramids of Teotihuacán. When we climb to the top of them, experiencing, with all the effort in our body, our insignificance, we see how their low-rising forms correspond to the distant hills, such that they express not the will and ostentation of a human ruler but the immemorial presence of rock, sun, and moon. There is no grandeur in the great size of the palace of Charles V in the Alhambra, whose square bulk brutally disrupts the harmony of the Nasrid palaces, terraces, and gardens, and the snow-covered mountains behind.

There is dominion in the erratic lines and forms of a cliff that astonish us with the boundless production of forms in mineral forces. There is sovereignty in the turbulent forces of an ocean storm. We see something sublime in the pale white filament roots of a mushroom that has hoisted up a slab of the sidewalk.

Importance is perceived in a vision of scope and sway and felt in what Nietzsche called "the pathos of distance."[2] In the Hagia Sofia the dimensions of the Byzantine world, its sense of the heights and depths of reality, its directives toward triumph and toward abjection, were first set up and can be seen yet today. The great ruby-red rock Uluru commands the endless flat deserts of central Australia like the very heart of the continent. One person, the one she loves, illuminates with his appreciating, graceful, and exhilarating gaze everything that she sees and touches. Before a frail wildflower in the forest we sense with pathos the immensity of forces about it that threaten it. We envision the unending desolation of time deprived of a species of crane in imminent danger of extinction.

Martin Heidegger replaced the substantive account of things with a relational account; what we discover of things, he said, is not "properties," that is, traits that belong to them, but "appropriatenesses"—concrete ways they fit into or resist other things about them and fit into our projects.[3] But the sublimity of things and events is recognized in the way they exceed concepts that measure their appropriateness to our projects. Their size, force, splendor, and wild freedom make them insubordinate to the uses we may devise for them.

"That's not just timber—that's a sequoia forest!" declares the utter disproportion between the concept that subordinates the trees to human uses and the perception of all their reality. The sublimity of the sequoia forest shows itself in the skyward thrust of the trees that elevates our eyes and lifts us from all that is heavy and depressed; it shows itself when we come to understand their immense age, their force that withstands all other forces—for nothing, not lightning that has struck them all and burned out the deadwood of their cores, not disease, not drought, nothing until men invented chain saws, can kill a sequoia. The splendor of a hummingbird shows itself in the elegance of its form and the intricacy of its movements, in its extraordinary force (hummingbirds, fluttering their wings seventy times a second, have a muscular strength exceeding any other known organism),[4] and in the vivacity of its sensitivity, seeing and tasting what our crude senses can hardly guess at.

* * *

Yet is there anything more subject to dispute than importance?

The disputes are resolved by broadening, deepening, and enriching our knowledge of that to which importance is attested. "You can't do that! That's a child!" "A child? This brat, this gangster!" The shopkeeper, beating up an adolescent thief, claims knowledge—of slum kids, of this kid. The social worker, in protesting, claims knowledge—of feelings and drives in this child that will not respond with the cowed obsequiousness the shopkeeper aims to produce with his beatings and also of feelings and drives in this child that, just as in other children, in the shopkeeper's children, can be elicited by humane actions. To argue for an end to witch burnings, slavery, the oppression of sexual minorities, we argue that the information that is broadcast about them is false and we seek to replace it with true. To convince people that the wetlands must be protected, we lead them to compare a geologic and biological diversity that maintains itself and thrives with the laterite wasteland left after a few individuals got their short-term private gain.

But isn't importance *ascribed* to things? In ordinary language, importance is said to be ascribed when what is taken to be important we deem not really important. "He acts as though ingratiating the higher-ups is the most important thing in the world." "What importance she is attributing to a mere diploma!"

Some theorists, however, have come to think with David Hume[5] that values cannot be derived from facts, and hence all importance is ascribed by human agents to persons, other animal species, ecological systems, artworks, and buildings that cannot strictly speaking be said to have importance. This supposes that we have available a perception and a description of the surroundings in which we act and refrain from acting that is value-free. These theorists assume that such a description exists in the discourses of the various natural sciences. However, the alleged pure facts formulated in chemistry, astronomy, or biology are constructed with inevitable elements of theory, and they implicate theoretical values such as simplicity and scope as well as predictability and technological usefulness. In addition, the environment as formulated by chemistry or biology is not that in which we act, and it is not that in which a biochemist acts when she drives her Jeep down a path to try to locate some ore-bearing rocks or study a stretch of wetlands. The notion of importance includes an original perception of importance in things and is enriched by subsequent such perceptions.

Immanuel Kant recognized intrinsic importance in our rational faculty. He argues that as soon as thought arises, it finds it has to conceive things correctly and reason rightly: it must conceive for things coherent and consistent concepts. The necessity for thought to conceive coherent and consistent concepts maintains it in exercise in all situations. In order to conceive things correctly and reason rightly, we must move toward and around things so as to perceive them in ways that lend themselves to coherent concepts. The imperative weighing on thought must become practical: it must command our sensory and practical powers. Thought does not derive its importance from its evolutionary or pragmatic usefulness.

Kant does not recognize intrinsic importance in the material things about us or even in our life. Food, drink, and shelter are means for living. However, living is not imposed on us as imperative, Kant observes, since unsatisfied want and need could instead motivate suicide and do so. What alone could make it necessary for us to live, Kant argues, is the intrinsic importance of the rational faculty in us. Actions are to be judged by their rationality.[6]

For Kant, the pyramids of Egypt, cliffs in the Alps, storms at sea, and the stars of the night skies are not themselves sublime. Instead, their great size and complexity and the immensity of their forces, exceeding what our eyes can encompass and measure, provoke our mind to conceive the idea of infinity. And it is our mind's own power to conceive the idea of infinity, Kant claims, that arouses the feeling of the sublime.[7]

In giving intrinsic importance exclusively to the rational mind, Kant fails to understand other animals, ecological systems, artworks, or buildings with perceptual and conceptual sensitivity, logical acumen, and breadth and depth of comprehension.

To see is to see what can be done. To see something is to see how it could be explored. To see something's importance is to see how we must abide with it, how we must hike the wilderness, live near and for the wilderness, how we must honor dance and how we must dance. To see what a thing is in itself is to see what it requires. Our action is mobilized by the perception of something to be preserved, repaired, rescued, or supplemented: our lives, what is important in our lives, and what is important in itself. The importance recognized in a person, animal, inert object, or artwork directs our action, prohibits some actions, perhaps imposes nonaction.

From the importance of freedom from hunger and sickness, of freedom from tyrants and exploiters, a dominant tradition in Western thought had erected freedom as the supreme value sought in all human action. To find ourselves not ordered or directed from the outside would be the most spiritual state and the condition for independent thought, artistic creation, personal work, and the sense of self-worth and pride. Yet thoughts are not produced by freely willing them; they occur to a thinker when they will. When a thought does come, a thinker follows when and where it leads, its exhilarated servant. It did not occur to Beethoven to want to be free to compose or not compose the music he continued to compose long after he could no longer hear it. A craftsman prizes supremely the craft to which he finds his resources and skills destined, not the freedom to practice it or not. To find ourselves in love is to find ourselves not free but captivated. Indeed, are not the deciding encounters of our lives events whose necessity we did not perceive in the determinisms of nature or the institutions and procedures of the economic and social field? We are guided by signs and omens: we intuit directives in chance events.

In what we do, we respond to directives that are visible in things. For craftsmen there is a right way to make something and a right way to use each thing. Hang gliders learn from the winds and the thermals and from the materials the right way to make and to fly a hang glider, as a composer learns from the symphony emerging before her which are not yet the right notes. Explorers of microcosms and macrocosms devote their minds to them like dancers to the score and calibrate their sense organs and manual skills to their instruments like performers to the keyboard and pedals of a cathedral organ. The more vast and baffling the problem—armed conflicts between peoples that have lasted for generations, the destruction of Earth's ozone shield and global warming, the formation of galaxies millions of light years ago and the events in the first seconds of the cosmic Big Bang—the more there arise people who find in it a summons for their minds, their passions, and their skills.

As for performers there are the right feelings to find for every turn in the score of the concerto and dance, there are the right feelings for an ancient ritual in a sacred place, for the Colca Canyon, and for condors and lemurs. Every sensualist knows that there is a right way to savor the wine and the perfumes of a tropical garden, a right way to move in the rain forest and see the moths dance and to watch the night come upon the mountain town.

To perceive the importance of things that have to be protected, nurtured, or rescued is to perceive what has to be done. What has to be done becomes what I have to do, when what has to be done is urgent and I am the one who is there and has the resources.

Kant identified as "categorically imperative" the case where I find that I have compelling and urgent reason to do something, whatever I may happen to want to do. What I have to do is "hypothetically imperative" when it depends on my inclinations, desires, and goals. When what we have to do is categorically imperative, Kant says, our will acts alone and suppresses our inclinations, our desires, and our own goals.[8]

But our desires and inclinations drive our responses once an objective becomes our objective. If we not only recognize what we have to do but do it, we will do it because the importance of what has to be preserved, repaired, or rescued awakens inclinations and loyalties in that long-range orientation of our life that is called our character. The doctor on vacation who identifies herself when a child suffers an epileptic seizure does so because she wants to be a healer more than she wants to lie dreamily on the beach. If we recognize that we have to give a lift to this lovesick man in Port-au-Prince whose lover is in Souvenance, this recognition comes from the inward vision cherishing a life sovereignty driven by passion, a vision that is stabilized as our character.

The men put only women and children on the lifeboats and stayed on board as the *Titanic* sank. Is that not because care for the weak and a sense of honor had long been integrated into their character—and because the courage of their mates strengthened them in the throes of terror? We refuse to lie, even to save our life. A captured guerilla refuses to disown her convictions even under torture because she has consecrated her life to the cause. An arrested rapist confesses out of disgust with his act.

How often is what we think we want determined by training, habit, lack of imagination, or obscure and unconscious fears! How agitated or how indolent we are, without ever getting a sense of what we want! How much of what we do we do only to make the time pass! We do things to make the time pass until a friend comes, until we get sleepy enough to go to bed, to get through the summer, to fill up retirement—and find that we never did anything we really wanted to do. Do we not discover what we want to do only when we discover what we have to do?

In conducting the diving expedition with all the knowledge and skill the piloting of the boat and the handling of the scuba equipment require, and in ensuring that those on the expedition are reassured against mishaps and shown how to see the denizens of the ocean, the dive master finds that being a dive master is what he really wants to do. In leaving highly paid private nursing for the pampered rich to care for the wounded and the famished in a refugee camp, a nurse finds that she is doing what she really wants to do.

8

I am a . . .

When we speak about things, they become clearer; they break apart or connect up differently; words may well make things and situations first appear. Words also present the speaker. "Here I am!" "I saw, I heard, I did . . ." "I say, I tell you . . ." The "I" presents the speaker and maintains him or her present.

Linguistics has labeled the word "I" an empty "shifter"; it designates the one who is now uttering this phrase and in the course of a conversation it designates first this person, then that person, then that other person. Literary critics have pointed out that the word "I" in a text can designate the author of that text, or the narrator in a novel who puts himself forth as having seen these events or lived through them, or a fictitious speaker to whom the author has ascribed certain states of mind and actions.

What I ascribe to the word "I" when I use it can be the same as what anyone else ascribes to it: "She is the thirteenth on the wait list for that flight." "I am the thirteenth in line for that flight."

But there are instances where the word "I" has a special force. "I am on my own now." "I am a mother." When, alone or in the presence of others, she says "I," she impresses it upon herself, and her substance retains it. With these words, she takes a stand and faces ahead. The next time she says "I," this subsequent "I" corresponds to and answers for the prior one.

"I got mad when my petition was just ignored . . ." "I am so happy I quit my job." With these words, the present I puts the past I in the present I. The I that quit or that got mad is the I that is now speaking.

The power to fix my own word on myself is a power that leaps over the succession of hours and days to determine the future now. One day, deep in the secrecy of my heart, I said, "I am a dancer," and it is because and only because I uttered those words that I am now on the way to becoming a dancer. Already to say "I am a man" is to commit myself to manly behavior; to say "I am a woman" is to commit myself to womanly deeds. To say "I am young still" is to put my forces outside the roles and role models set up about me.

The remembering of these words that we implant in ourselves is made possible by brushing off the thousands of impressions that crowd on our sensory surfaces as we move through the thick of the world. The

I arises in an awakening, out of the drowsy murmur of sensations. It especially requires an active forgetting of lapses, failures, and chagrins—which persist as cloying sensations that mire our view, occluding the past and the path ahead. There is a fundamental innocence in the I, which stands in the now and from this clearing turns to the time ahead and the time passed. To say "I" is to commence. "Now I see!" "I will go!" There is youth and adventure in the voice that says "I."

"Now I see!" These words, once I fixed them in myself, leave me free to observe the passing scene without tentatively arranging it around one center and then around another. "I will go" leaves me free for whatever interruptions, distractions, and momentary amusements the day brings. Through innumerable interruptions, contraventions, invitations, and lures to do other things, I feel the uncanny power of these words that is the sole evidence that they will prevail.

"Now I see!" "I am still young." To utter "I" is to pledge to honor those words. Nobility characterizes, in someone of high station or of low, the man who is as good as his word, the woman whose word is a guarantee. Servile is he whose words are not his own, she who is not in her actions.

Our word "I," "I say . . . ," "I am going to . . . ," "I am a . . ." is the first and fundamental way we honor ourselves. Saying "I am a dancer," I will seek out dance classes, I will train every day with exclusive resolve, I will endure being left out of company selections, dancing in troupes that get miserable reviews by the critics; I will never act on the basis of failure. It is myself, and not dance, I dishonor if I do not do these things.

The word of honor we have fixed in ourselves is the real voice of conscience. Already "Now I see!" or "I have no idea what to do with my life" are words that remain in me, that orient and direct my words and deeds.

Our dancer conscience is not at all a critical function, a restraining force, like the daemon of Socrates, which speaks only to say no to the instincts. Our artist conscience does not torment us with guilt feelings. In the words "I am a dancer!" "I am a mother!" "I am young still!" we feel surging power. Our pride in ourselves is a trust in the power of these words. There is a trembling pulse of joy in those words and a foretaste of joy to come. We trust our joy, for joy is expansive, opening wide upon what is, what happens, and it illuminates most broadly and most deeply.

The word we have put on ourselves is fixed in our sensibility, our nervous circuitry, our circadian rhythms, and our momentum and its tempo. It vanishes from the conscious mind, which can fill itself with new words and scenarios. I no longer have to recall, in the midst of morning concerns that require my attention, that word "dancer" uttered in myself; I instinctually head for the dance studio and feel restless and tied down if I am prevented from going.

* * *

The chance revelation of the importance of dance, the grandeur of the wilderness, the majesty of the oceans first called forth the words—"I am a dancer!" "I am a forester!" "I am an oceanographer!"—with which I passionately endorsed and committed myself to these experiences. The enchanting force of the word "dancer" resonates with the mesmerizing force of dance that has impassioned me. There is gratitude in being able to affirm these words.

To be struck by the importance of dance, of mothering a child, or of freeing the rivers of pollution is to see the urgency of what has to be brought about, protected, rescued, or repaired. Seeing that I am the one who is there and who has the resources, the I arises and takes a stand.

To say "I am a dancer" is to commit my body to travail, injury, and pain. To say "I am a mother" is to commit my body to set free the child, and the adolescent and adult it bore, or to care for the genetically defective child it gave birth to until its death. To say "I am a doctor" is to commit my body to total mobilization for hours and at any hour and to the daily proximity to deadly diseases.

And how much more strength is required to say "I am an explorer of myself by being an explorer of a hundred towns and lands!" How rigorous is the conscience of him who affirms, "I am someone who risks all that I am in every new land and adventure!" But to be really a dancer is to be a runaway youth on an unknown road, to be, like Martha Graham, a beginner at the age of eighty. To be a mother can be, like Celia de la Serna, to be dragged out of the cancer ward and thrown in prison in Buenos Aires for being the mother of her son, the mother of Ernesto "Che" Guevara.

This power to fix our word in ourselves generates the power, Nietzsche said, "to see distant eventualities as if they belonged to the present, to decide with certainty what is the goal and what the means to it, to distinguish necessary events from chance ones, to think causally, and in general to be able to calculate and compute."[1] How many are those who do not distinguish what is essential from what is incidental, who do not see what possibilities are within reach and do not even see goals! How many are those who do not think, whose minds are but substances that record what baits and lures the communications industry broadcasts at large! They do not commit themselves to the systems of thought that track down the causes of injustice and sociopathic behavior, the causes of environmental deterioration, the causes of literary and artistic achievement.

Compelling insights, foresight, purposive thought, causal thought, calculative thought—thought in general—these do not arise from the regularities of nature passively recorded by the mind. The rows of trees and the daily movement of clouds overhead, the birds that chatter in the backyard, the landmarks and the paths we take every day, the tasks that are laid out for us every day, the patterns of conversation with acquaintances, the concepts that exist to classify these things and the connections between them—these lull the mind, which glows feebly in their continuities and recurrences; they do not make it thoughtful. Thought results from language, thought arises out of the word we put on ourselves—a word of honor. This word interrupts the continuities of nature and silences the babble of others in us. The power that we feel in ourselves when we fix ourselves with a word, that stands and advances in that word, the feeling that we are making our nature determinable, steadfast, trustworthy, makes us look for regularities, necessities, calculable forms in the flux of external nature. Once I have said, "I will be a dancer," I begin to really determine what the things about me are; I begin to understand anatomy, the effects of exercise, of diet, the effects of great teachers and grand models, the workings of a whole cross section of urban society. It is the man of his word, the woman whose word is a guarantee, who is thoughtful.

To say "I" is to disconnect myself from the others, the crowd, the company, the system. It is to disconnect myself from their past and their future. "For my part, I think . . ." "Here is what I am going to do . . ." I disconnect from the view another may have of me and the image I have constructed of him, and from the interpretation he may have elaborated of what I said. "Yes, I did say I would clear up the place before the social worker got here. So what? I am no longer the suburban housewife you knew."

Because the utterance "I" is a commitment, it is also the power to disconnect myself from a past experience, undertaking, or commitment. "I didn't see what was going on." "I was drunk." "Oh I was so much older then. I'm younger than that now." And it is also the power to disconnect myself from the future that was mine. "The troops are already shelling the village and you say they are going to level it? Well, I am a doctor and I am staying right here to tend to the dying."

To say "I" is to disconnect myself from the others and from discourse with others. "Now I see," I say in the middle of a discussion, and I may stay in the discussion to argue for what I see and try to affect the subsequent movement of their thoughts and their decisions. More likely, the main effect of my insight will be to determine the line of my thoughts and decisions after I leave the others. My word of honor does not get its meaning from a dialectic, and its use is not primarily in a language game with others. He who goes around saying to everyone "I'm going to be a dancer" is seeking their permission and support, and there is cause to suspect that he has not really or not yet fixed these words in his heart. There are those who have never told anyone and who are driven by their secret intoxication with this word. Secrecy sets this word apart from the profane common talk; it sacralizes it. Secrecy also maintains for us a space for giving free play to doubts, second thoughts about what we have said to ourselves, as well as giving free play to fantasy about it.

The walls of secrecy fragment our social identity. He who has said in his heart "I am a dancer" will not be the same person among his fellow prelaw students in the university, before his parents, when seeking private lessons from a renowned teacher, when playing football with cousins at the family reunion. The secrecy of our words can function to preserve affable and nonconfrontational relations with others who have different commitments and those who have different plans for us.

To say "I am a dancer" is not to impose upon myself an overall coherence and cohesion. In the heart of myself I am a dancer; but the whole of what I am is a singular compound of fragmentary systems of knowledge, incomplete stocks of information and discontinuous paradigms, disjoint fantasy fields, personal repetition cycles, and intermittent rituals. Inner walls of secrecy maintain a space where quite discontinuous, noncoordinated, noncommunicating psychic systems can coexist.

How do I understand that I came to believe that I am destined to be a dancer? How do I explain it out of the segments of information I acquired about the social and cultural structures about me, the successive role models that I fixed in memory, the fantasies of my childhood, the resentments and rebellions I accumulated against my parents, the ways I came to disdain pragmatic judgments and occupations? But I may not want to penetrate behind those walls about my dancer destiny: let this word "dancer!" be separated and secret—sacred. Saying yes to the enigmas and accepting the discomfiture within myself, I remain astonished at the Dionysian demon that has come to possess me.

One will not become a dancer unless one says, "I am a dancer"; one will not become an adventurer unless one says, "I am a adventurer." But I will not become a dancer or an adventurer unless I believe what I say in my heart. By an act of will I may want to be a dancer, but I do not by an act of will make myself believe that I am a dancer.

Is not belief in oneself one of those states that cannot be brought about intentionally or willfully? I can make myself eat with an act of will, but I cannot with an act of will make myself hungry; I can make myself go to bed but cannot make myself sleepy, can willfully bring about self-assertion or bravado but not courage, meekness but not humility, envy but not lust, commiseration but not sympathy, congratulations but not admiration, reading but not understanding, knowledge but not wisdom.[2] I cannot by an act of will make myself be amused; I cannot make myself laugh by tickling myself.

The word of honor that we fix on ourselves that makes us thoughtful also makes us insightful. In uttering "I," I make myself present—present to things and events where and as they are. To say "I," to say "Here I am," is to commence to see lucidly where and what here is; to say "Now I see" is to put myself in the clear light that illuminates what is ahead; to say "I am a dancer" is to know what dance is, is to know dance taking possession of myself and activating my nervous circuitry and musculature with its rigorous dynamics.

What is revealed in an impassioned experience is sudden and unexpected, revealed to us gratuitously. The revelation of dance reveals in us the capacity and the latent talent to dance; the revelation of the healing powers of medicine reveals in us skills, perceptiveness, focus that we consecrate in saying "I am a doctor!" They reveal what we are, by nature and by chance, by luck. All the good things in life are free.

To believe something is to be compelled to hold that belief because there is evidence that it is true. A patient is told she has cancer. Believing that there is no hope will certainly depress the immune system. She has to believe that there is hope. But how to make herself believe there is hope? Is there any other way than to find reasons to believe that chemotherapy and radiation treatments or the treatments used in Chinese hospitals are effective?

Paul Gauguin abandoned his family in order to pursue his art. "I am moving next month to Fatu-iva, a still almost cannibalistic island in the Marquesas. There, I feel, completely uncivilized surroundings and total solitude will revive in me, before I die, a last spark of enthusiasm which will rekindle my imagination and bring my talent to its conclusion."[3] He did have reason to believe that he had talent. He did not know if he could bring that talent to its conclusion. If the ship, on its long voyage through stormy seas, would not arrive, if he had succumbed to disease on the way, no one would ever have known.

Here is this man who has fallen ill with a strange sickness or into a deep depression. He suffers and seeks to be healed. But strange illness, depressions, hallucinations are part of the initiation of every shaman. What might happen is that he becomes a healer. How to know that this is his destiny? I. M. Lewis and Georges Devereux reclassified shamans as neurotics. But neurotics are dysfunctional in our culture and shamans do heal dysfunctional individuals in their cultures. Field researchers have long observed shamans performing tricks—pulling out of the sick person's body the cause of the sickness, a bloody object that he had furtively put there. Does the shaman who makes others believe in his healing powers believe in them himself or make himself believe in them? Shamans recognize that there are charlatans, all of whose healing is a sham. They also see people they treat getting well.

This pastor in Northern Ireland or Rwanda—does he really believe that all things are in the hands of an omnipotent and benevolent Divine Providence? Does this man passing as normal really believe he is normal? Is it not by passing as heterosexual that we quit our bisexual preadolescence or indeed nature? Nietzsche observed that the noble always go masked, masked as noble.[4]

David Abram is a young American who was working his way through college putting on magic shows. When he finished, he applied for and received a number of small grants to study magic in old cultures. He went to Sri Lanka, Bali, and Nepal. In fact, there are no magicians in those places; there are shamans and healers. In Bali he formed a relationship with a healer. She revealed to him some of the power objects and rituals of Bali. She intimated that he should share some of his powers with her. He tried to explain to her that he had no power; all he had were prestidigitation and tricks. But the concept of a magician in the Western sense was alien to her and her culture. Finally he realized that if he did not share something, she would shut him out and he would lose the person from whom he was learning most. This woman had some time back broken her thumb, which had set badly so that it had lost mobility. For her it was a serious debility, because she earned her income by the practice of massage—the healing was, in the culture, done without charge. One night things came to a head; David had to do something. He improvised a ritual over her hand, using some of the power objects of the culture. To his consternation, the next day she showed him how her thumb was beginning to regain mobility, and insisted he repeat the ritual. To his horror, in the days that followed, the thumb recovered completely.[5]

The hang glider who on his first leap off the cliff crashed on the rocks below knows he must immediately, the same day, leap off that cliff again until he soars in the winds. The day will come when soaring will have shown him pretty much all it can, and he will cease and go on to other explorations. But if he stops before he has overcome the cliff, he will have definitively reduced belief in his powers.

Cowardice, which husbands our forces, holds back, intensifying the sense of our needs and wants, produces an inward sense of impotence and misery. Every misery we feel over ourselves is the result of some cowardice.

* * *

Because she said I am a dancer and believed it, she could become a dancer. Can she be deluded? Can she even be lying to herself?

In the dance studio she found she really belonged there, her body belonged. If doubt arises, it is because she finds reasons and evidence for those reasons to think that she cannot be a dancer. Out of fear of the truth, she can hold back from looking for those reasons and that evidence. She can selectively scan the evidence, selectively weigh it, evaluate new pieces of evidence separately rather than cumulatively, or fail to take in negative evidence.[6] Later, she says, "I was deluding myself."

We do not really knowingly mislead ourselves. What is possible is that we may lack evidence or lack the ability to evaluate the evidence. What could count as decisive evidence that I will never be a dancer?

Yet do we not honor those who are true to the word they have given, although they are deluded about their talent or resources or about the importance or validity of the cause? It is not only historians who work to recuperate the honor of all the losers of history—Brutus and Montezuma, Gandhi and Che Guevara. The victors do not desecrate but bury in cemeteries their fallen enemies and receive with military honors the officers who, their cause lost, come to surrender.

In reality there is no honor in delusion. I will not be able to continue, having one day recognized that I have no talent, that I am not a dancer. I can recognize no honor in representing the party, once I learn that it has become corrupt and its program is now only propaganda.

If we continue to fight for a cause we know is lost, we do so to demonstrate to ourselves and our comrades and to those as yet unborn that the cause that is winning is ignoble.

Part 4

Visions

9

Our Visionary Body

To see the door or the park bench, we have to position our body, focus our eyes, and circumscribe its contours with our look. To hear a friend's voice in a restaurant, we have to turn our head toward him. To feel the give and softness of the velvet or the solidity and grain of a pine board, our hand strokes it with a corresponding pressure, rhythm, and range of movement. Our body's stance at any moment is not simply the resultant of the positions of the parts, each determined by the force of gravity and the outside pressures and internal tensions; there is an internal diagram that orients our body toward its task or objective and positions its limbs and sensory surfaces. Balance and orientation are maintained as a shift of position of one hand or leg induces a systematic shift in the positions of the others.

As we get out of bed, brush our teeth, and prepare breakfast, we have an inner sense of the overall axis and orientation of our body. While seated at a computer or operating machinery on our job, we are aware of the position of our legs and hands without looking at them. Making our way through a crowd or through the narrow turns of a cave, we sense the volume our body is occupying. This awareness is not the result of observation; it is produced by taking up positions and enacting movements. In the measure that we relax completely and let our arms and legs settle by gravity, our sense of their positions and contours fades out.

As an axis of posture takes form in our body, it emanates an image of itself as it would be seen from the outside. As we stretch our legs under the table, we have a sense of their shape and position in the visible room. When we stride down the boulevard, we do not only see parts of our legs and hands; we have a quasi-visual image of our whole body and gait as they would look to eyes stationed at a distance.[1] While we hurriedly weave our way through the crowded street, we have a sense of the thickness and thrust of our limbs as they would be felt by others whom we would brush against or who could crowd us. As we speak, we have a sense of the sound of our voice as it would be heard in the space outside. Having sprained our ankle, we lean against a friend to walk, and we have a sense of the weight of our body; when we walk across the seedling grass and climb the ladder, we have a sense of the weight of our body as it would be felt by the grass and the ladder.

In going to sleep, our bodies disconnect from implements and utilitarian postures; our head, settled on the pillow, anchors our body on the support and tranquillity of the ground. Our limbs and organs disconnect from the postural axis and generate images of themselves. Sigmund Freud found that in dreams the stirring and arousal of penises and vaginas elaborate the most far-fetched disguises—obelisks, knives, buildings, caves. But eyes, jaws, fists, and stomach are equally cores and source-points of our dreams, glittering as stars, hardened into traps and bludgeons, opened upon rivers and banquets. Banal or arcane dream images are combined and transformed by the lascivious, hungry, voracious, orgasmic, and discharging impulses of body parts. It is not our minds detached from our sleeping bodies, but our eyes, lips, jaws, teeth, fists, thighs, penises, clitorises, and vaginas that are generating images, are dreaming.

The psychoanalytic theory of introjection offers an explanation for the obelisks, caves, stars, traps, and bludgeons that are attached to body parts in dreams. In the first months of life, an infant progressively mobilizes and explores his body, which becomes more and more distinct and separate from the arms and body of his mother and from outlying things that have places of their own. He defends himself against the diffuse pressure of the environment by detaching some object from it, bringing it inside, and closing himself against the rest. It is not simply that sounds reverberate and colored patterns hover in the inner space of his body; the infant brings whole objects into it. He feels occupied, tormented by objects he has introjected.

The infant's inner space is not a sealed capsule where a selfsame core ego would abide. Infantile "fantasizing" is not a projection of images without substance or force generated by an idling mind. The infant's ability to hold on to some introjected object and close himself against the rest produces a sense of inwardness and gives him a pleasurable sense of substantiality, while the pressure of the introjected object makes him feel vulnerable and suffering. Infantile fantasies are not simple gratifications of wish fulfillment; introjection maintains in the infant a "paranoid-schizoid position."[2]

In sleep this inner space is dismembered. The body parts and organs intensify their spaces by introjecting the objects that torment them and that attract contiguous or remote objects that separate and overlap, leap, collide, and shatter in the theater of dreams.

Our bodies regularly produce excess energies that have to be released. They seek out contact with beings closed in themselves, not neutralized by the comprehensive appropriation of our understanding, not subjected to our forces and our uses, incomprehensible or absurd, wild and free. Impassioned states are produced when some introjected object becomes so vehement and aggravating that the inner hold on it breaks down, releasing an onrush of free energies.

Sexual arousal does not simply issue in the swelling and lubricating of the genital organs and the release of physical compulsions; it generates erotic images. In solitary sexual pleasuring of our body there is a torrid presence of imagined sexual partners and a scenario of seduction; in sexual interplay with another fully present and denuded in our arms the partner is transfigured, mythologized, and the situation dramatized.[3] The partner is not only a human female or male but a fox, harlot, goddess, mother, earth mother; a wolf or libertine, Jesus or Thor. The pressure of multiple beings introjected releases voluptuous energies in a collapse of our stabilized psychic structures. The breakdown of inner integrity and control makes sexual excitement an ecstatic torment.

Finding ourselves slighted, thwarted, or struck without being able to deliver a riposte at once, or to engage our powers and energies in a task or a conversation in which we are master, can leave us with excess energies unoccupied. This state becomes wrathful as we detach the adversary, hold on to him with all our forces, aggravating his presence inside, and introject other forms—sneak, gangster, mafioso, tyrant, pig—with which to hold him but also to increase the morose intensity.

Outbursts of joy are visionary. Awakening to the Antarctic dawn blazing unnamable colors and forms in the ice fields or seeing emerging from the airplane our lover returning from a long absence releases a flood of ecstatic energies that overwhelms our sense of ourselves. To take hold of the presence invading us, we introject fantastic figures from childhood, from myths and legends, experiencing then more intensely their vehement and uncontainable presence.

In the impassioned experience in which I say "I am a dancer," dance invades me, occupies me, obsesses me. The physical skills and psychic, cognitive, and social structures successively elaborated since childhood that stabilized my identity break down in an onrush of energies committed to becoming a dancer. Within, dance generates visions of studios, great dancers, inspired teachers, visions of dances never yet enacted, a world where "all things themselves are dancing: they come and offer their hands and laugh and flee—and come back."[4]

Oracular Words

Words have forms; they receive their sense and function from the contrasts they mark within a constellation of words. They are relays; they connect up with other words, articulating things and events in more detail, connecting them with things and events that explain them, mapping them on other situations and at other times. They exist in movement.

Words have force: they intensify what they recognize. "A giant sequoia!" "A leafy dragonfish!" "A historic event!" "A catastrophe!" Noble words ennoble, beautiful words enhance, strong words empower, commonplace words trivialize, healthy words invigorate, sick words enfeeble what we confront and us in uttering them.

In impassioned experiences, the voice that consecrates with noble words what rises before us affirms and safeguards it and lets it spread its force in our words. "How grand are the sequoia forests!" "What integrity and courage in these destitute refugees!" "How venal this extermination of the endemic wildlife!" Curses arise from the inner forces that have run up against the malignant and malevolent and intensify both the strength of our repugnance and the sway of the evil itself.

Psychoanalysis takes the images of our dreams and daydreams to be "structured like a language." They can be translated into words and phrases. Conversely, words emanate images. The surface we see shows us the wall; the sound we hear materializes the shattering glass, the cart rumbling over the cobblestones, the distress and terror of someone in the night. Words too call up visions of things imminent or far-off.[1] Brief words—"dance," "mother," "on the road"—reverberate in the distances and in depth, striking up luminous apparitions and destinies.

The words with which others identify us—"Jean is a man," "She is the mother," "He is a pilot"—may function simply to identify us with a category, situate us in a class or social function. But in pronouncing inwardly or out loud the words "I am a man," "I am a dancer," "I am a mother," I stand forth. Fixed in myself, these commonest of words generate visions of things not yet seen, of open roads and wilderness beyond the corporate post at which we are stationed, of dances never yet seen or danced in a world where all things are dancing, of the orphaned HIV-positive child we held in our arms in Ethiopia. In our visionary body, the word we put on ourselves in saying "as for me," "I, a mother," "I am young still," is an oracular word.

Part 5

The Story of the I

11

Chronicle and Story

Once we have affirmed "I am a dancer" or "I am a mother," we have something to tell, which is not just the anonymous and haphazard course of events beginning with the dumb fact of our conception and birth.[1] We see and tell, first to ourselves, where we came from, how we came to be here and to be a primatologist, a sexual outlaw. We hold on to the impassioned experience that shimmers with visions of remote and portentous things and events, and we map out our situation and our resources.

It is a story, not simply our life plan, that we tell ourselves.[2] A story is dramatic; its episodes are apparitions, excitements, risks, and adventures. The events of the story are determined not by the laws governing the causality of nature and our nature but by our visions and the omens and portents they cast before and behind us. The story recounts stretches of exasperated frustration, forced detours, dead ends, and windfalls; unexpected breakthroughs, unforeseen triumphs, and the gnawing anxiety that such triumphs may never come again. Our story integrates them into our identity: I am a mother; in a chance visit to a refugee camp I adopted this orphan. I am a journalist who finally was able to tell the real story of the inner city. I am a revolutionary whose struggle was crushed. I am a dreamer who settled down. We can tell ourselves that our story is the story of everyman, or of a mass of mindless particles passing other masses with the same kind of insignificance that other clouds of mindless particles have in outer space. Those who say "My life is shit" or "Me—I'm nothing" say so out of the story they tell themselves.

Our story is not a chronicle of our lives; much is left out: the continuity and regularity of ordinary life, events that left us indifferent. Whole stretches of our lives may appear to us as distractions or as times when nothing really happened.

Our experiences break with the continuity and regularity of ordinary life, but our story acquires a rhythmic character. Our experiences figure as motif and counterpoint. Periodically we retell our story to ourselves.

Know thyself! Socrates enjoined—but we do not know ourselves by conceptualizing our decisions and actions in rational and explanatory schemata. New experiences, however unforeseeable and baffling, and the impassioned states they arouse, will be shaped by the story that had preceded them. And they may induce us to realign the plot, introduce new characters, or even abandon our word of honor. As we project the plot of our lives into the coming days and years, we incorporate pure guesses, wishful thinking, and imaginative constructions.

We shift points of view and narrative voice; we incorporate into the story we tell ourselves our story as we hear others tell it. We insert it into or compare it with the plots of stories told of others in the newspapers, in the media, in literature, in the anonymous legends, myths, and epics of our culture.

Yet the story I tell myself about who I am and where is unlike any story ever told. I find that my situation, my vision, the accidents and windfalls on my path do not fit into the available cultural patterns of epic, opera, tragedy, romance, ballet, comedy, vaudeville, sitcom, or farce. With abashed wonder I recognize the chance to have been born in this time and place with these resources or to have been born at all. Even if I am everyman and no one, I am so in a here and now that has never before occurred and will never be repeated.

The story I tell myself of my experiences may remain secret, as may the word of honor I have put on myself. Or I may tell my story to others, to make clear to them who I am, to integrate my experiences with theirs so as to make clear our common predicament and resources, or simply to entertain them. Telling my story to others may well function to clarify it to myself and enable me to commit myself to what an impassioned experience showed me was important, map out my resources, and enable me to exult in my strengths and laugh over my bunglings, grieve and mourn, bless and curse.[3]

Philosophy from the beginning introduced an explanation of our actions in terms of final causes: that we move in this direction rather than that is to be explained by intentions and goals projected by our minds—futures conjured by our minds. The empirical sciences explain actions by physico-chemical, magnetic, and electrical impulses, instincts and drives, or social forces: present reactions are determined by past causes and conditions. Nietzsche explains the force of our actions and reactions by the internal buildup of excessive forces that have to be discharged, and the direction by the chance encounter with some event that releases their discharge. The intentions and goals contrived by the mind, he says, are assigned to our moves after the event to justify them to ourselves. The justification is chosen for its beauty rather than its truth.[4] Here is this woman whose family and career leave her with energies, a curious intelligence, a charged sensibility, and physical skills unoccupied. By chance she comes upon the plight of the great whales, threatened with extinction. Later, to explain, to justify, her work with the Save the Whales campaign, she speaks of finding her vocation and speaks of the nobility of that cause.

Nietzsche insisted on the aesthetic motive that governs the story that we tell of our lives. We willingly avow that we are not saints, we can accept that we are not good citizens, but we despise our lives if we cannot view them as tragic or comic, epic or charming, an adventure or a fugue. When we view our lives as muddled and repugnant, distasteful to ourselves, we become rancorous and vindictive. Nietzsche said that the one thing needful is that we find our lives agreeable to look at:[5] "We want to be the poets of our life—first of all in the smallest, most everyday matters."[6] What makes our lives have aesthetic value for us is style; we are pleased with the "classical" style of our strong and dominating character or by our wild, arbitrary, fantastic, disorderly, and surprising free nature.[7]

But the style we give to our lives—gracious and affable like society hostesses or ceremonious and pompous like the old kings Zarathustra encounters[8]—may not emerge from the paces of our impassioned experiences and from the rhythms and musicality of our natures. Whether we look upon our lives as important or not does not depend on the style only but of the importance of what we have encountered in our experiences. The Tuareg nomads of the Sahara, the San of the Kalahari Desert, and the Quechua of the Peruvian Andes live lives bereft of possessions and enacting immemorial patterns of movement and labor. But they are passionately attached to the rhythms of their nomadic movement in the grandeur of the desert or their sedentary labor in high mountains. Their way of life is as enchanting to them as the austere refrains of their ancestral songs.

It could well be that we are pleased with only episodes in our story. The notary is pleased only with the poetry of his youth; the mediocre libertine pleased only with the sultanas he dreamed of long ago.

There are dedramatizing styles that level the disruptions and the risk; telling ourselves that we are but a mass of mindless particles passing other such masses, we can trivialize whatever experiences were important. There are those who recognize that the story of their lives is but a story of trivial experiences, which they may seek to recast as amusing, charming, virtuous, or blessed.[9] Culture is well stocked with kitsch, with poster child citizens and oleograph saints.

12

Fabled Places

To see through the trees the village lights at the bottom of the valley is to see a half hour's walk ahead. We edge closer to the fly so that it cannot elude the speed of our hand and swatter. Places separated in space are distant in time.

We may first locate places with a map, with coordinates of longitude and latitude, with diagrams of the roads and the mileage marked on them. Then, as we come to inhabit places, they acquire narrative positions: this intersection is where the way to the mountain starts; that's the restaurant where we all got food poisoning. When we move into a new home, we seek out some stories about it: who lived here, who built it, how it had been burglarized, whether the hurricane damaged it. As a house becomes our home, its porch, its bedroom, its toilet, its front trees and back garden acquire stories.

The story we tell ourselves of our lives gives narrative locations of impassioned experiences to the landscape, the city or hamlet, the productive or unproductive industry, the politically administered region about us. The visible places are places where the visions that determined our lives occurred or places where our visions were clouded over or extinguished. It is not the bare material objects of our environment or the forces that we see in them but the storied place that provokes and shapes our actions. If the story we tell of our lives provokes us to leave this place, we do so because of the story embedded in this boomtown region without dance teachers and conservatories, of this industrializing zone where our family and clan were driven from ancestral lands.

When we return to the place of our childhood, we recognize the woods where we hid out for two days, the garage where we compared our body with our brother's. We come upon old stories in our environment: the mosque build by the Mogul emperor, the arrowheads made by the Illini Indians who perished on Starved Rock, the house on the edge of the woods that remains empty and where something must have happened. To walk the outer radius of the bomb exploded on Hiroshima is to recognize that we were supporters and beneficiaries of a mass incineration of civilians. To wander in the rain forests of Amazonia or cross the central deserts of Australia is to see the vine that from the canopy sent down aerial roots and finally strangled the hundred-foot-high tree, the storms that leveled vast swaths of the shallow-rooted tropical forest, the wind eroding the rocks and shifting the dunes, the cosmic epic of the wanderings and collisions of continental plates.

13

Wounds and Words

The process by which a wish, an insight, a feeling, even a negative thought or feeling, vocalized into song becomes a pleasure has, despite all its importance, thus far been beyond the reach of our neurology and psychology. The process by which a wound, a pain gives rise to vocalization is only apparently simple.

A wounded animal hisses, squeals, screams, or roars. The great energy of its vocalizations is threatening to an attacker. The outcries of a wounded young bird or mammal call for help from its parents; those of an adult call to the flock or herd for help. Birds and mammals (including humans) also mutter and whimper, moan and whine as the pain sets in and endures, though often their vulnerable situation counsels silence. Voltaire said that language has been given to humans so that they can dissimulate their thoughts, but in fact we have a natural impulse to say what we see and feel; we have to learn to lie. Wounds issue in vocalizations; we have to learn not to cry or moan when we hurt.

Pain is immanence; it is conscious, nothing but consciousness, a consciousness backed up to itself, mired in itself. To suffer pain is for consciousness to be unable to flee or retreat from itself, unable to project itself outside upon some outlying object or event. Suffering gives rise to whimperings, moanings, sobbings, and murmurings—typically rhythmic—with which the body mired in pain strives to reestablish internal kinetic melodies and with them make contact with the arpeggios and drumrolls of things passing outside.

The vocalizations of others can come to join this whimpering and moaning; their soothing murmurs and songs send their ripples into the turbid space of pain. For someone in pain, the sobbing and keening of onlookers amplifies the pain but amplifies also the vocalizations with which the sufferer's body seeks to reestablish its periodicities and kinetic melodies.

Wounds, pain, and suffering generate words. It is true that our vocabularies offer us but a limited list of words to describe our pain, as they offer us so few words to describe our pleasures. But wounds, pain, and suffering generate words to map out our reactions to them and the actions we have to undertake to foresee, avoid, repair, and heal them. We consult a doctor, and science takes over. The scientific discourse maps out genetic and biochemical deficiencies, bacteria or viruses that drifted in, or tumorous growths—events in a space without purpose and finality. The medical discourse draws up possible chemical or biochemical, genetic, or surgical interventions.

There is also among us an interpretative discourse, which aims to give meaning to our wounds and suffering and our mortality by evaluating their cause. It identifies incompetent doctors; uncomprehending, imprisoning, or castrating family members; irresponsible dieticians and medications; ignorant culinary traditions. It assigns culpability to the sick organism itself: counting on natural vigor, on the ability to recover from excesses, it has failed to care for itself properly. The suffering can then be interpreted as an admonition or a due punishment, in a social or cosmic space of finality and purpose.

How readily these words blaze into fulminations and accusations, intoxicated with their power! With them the sick body finds an authority it did not have when its youthful vitality made it curious and skeptical about all judgments. The requirements of convalescence, old age, and an ever-narrowing zone that we can manage hurl their needs as demands on the young and those with exuberant and far-ranging health. The sick incriminate their own organism inasmuch as it was moved by unbridled instincts and impulses—and is thus also an enemy to combat, to vanquish or control. This intelligence, ingenuity, craftiness, and cunning of interpretation have, from the age of Socrates and Euripides, proved powerful enough to assemble the bilious and morbid forces of the sick against the natural animal in us.

In the century and more since Nietzsche published *On the Genealogy of Morals*,[1] the moral discourse bent on giving a meaning to suffering and death has undergone repeated assaults, not the last by Susan Sontag in her *Illness as Metaphor*.[2] The medical discourse, not only of physical but also of mental suffering, alone reinforces its validity.

A sufferer, seeking to face the stern truth, learns this discourse. She learns its vocabulary and grammar so as to understand her doctors and communicate her observations to them. In this discourse she ceases to be a suffering individual to become a patient, passive and receptive, a case in a universe where her word of honor, commitments, and anxieties have no significance.

Yet, in order to live out her ordeal and her life as her own, the sufferer must acknowledge her debilitated or surgically mutilated body. She must bring to light what the medical discourse passes over: her shock, her fears, her hopes and despairs, her obduracy and cowardice. She must map out her infirmities and her capabilities for work, for sex, for companionship, for thought. This discourse will link present with past and future; it will be a story she tells to herself. "An illness faced down, transcended, or even talked to death," Paul West notes, "becomes a prized possession, first draft of a novel you cannot bear to destroy but keep by you to hearten and remind."[3]

West, suffering a massive heart attack, implantation of a pacemaker, and then diabetes, masters the medical discourse and also elaborates his own story. He describes his body as an electrochemical contraption whose composition is as randomly material as that of the effusions out of which the stars form, and he describes his death as a fall of a material mass down the chute to the refrigerators of the morgue in the hospital basement. He masters every detail of the material and functioning of the pacemaker to be inserted into the left ventricle of his heart. He uses the medical discourse in mapping out how to reprogram his days and movements around microwave ovens, burglar alarms, arc welding units, power tools, induction furnaces, library checkout mechanisms. But to accept the pacemaker, he would have to tell a story of his own about it.

> [The surgeon] would slide the probe through a vein, and then the flanges would bend back along the lead, giving way easily as the probe passed from the vein into the right atrium, where much of my trouble was to begin with. . . . Once inside the ventricle, they were supposed to spring outward again to snag the soft pulp inside. . . . What set my teeth on edge was that slithering lead, when it went past the defenseless portals at my core, silver interloper where the sun had never shone and where there was never rest. . . . Round and round my mind went, repeating the abomination to exorcize it. Surely the lead would slip and then, like some zany butterfly, waft around, touching off twitches and convulsions wherever it landed, scraping and abrading, make me gasp. . . . My heart would be coddling a tiny propeller forever. . . . Then I realized that, instead of fending off all these images and tangents, I must allow them full play as my head's means of getting used to the idea; my imagination was translating for me, the barbaric into the tender, and I broke through to the palatable comparison that had been at the back of my mind all along. Instead of that chimney-brush lead, I was going to have the pink and velvet-gentle pistil of a hibiscus slid into my vein, with five red-spotted stamens in the vanguard, behind them the shank of the pistil and the tiny wire whisk of pliant golden commas that were the pollen.[4]

To reject the effort to make sense of our fate, to repudiate all moral interpretation of our suffering takes strength, the strength to throw off the authority the sick body gives to its recriminations. We find this strength in telling the story of the enigmatic and awesome health the body knew and still knows, which we did not create and do not comprehend.

> What all this "meant," I had no idea, and I still don't see why life, so long as we have it, should be "meaningful." We are here to bring our apparatus to bear, to pile up a mostly vanishing quota, say "thanks for the nice time," and go, which is why it seems to me worthwhile doing nothing more inventive than feeling my blood run, my eyes blink, my muscles twitch, all of these minima vaster than the nothing we go toward. We underestimate the delicious nullity of how things feel, in the body, when they're going right.[5]

The first draft of the novel the sufferer tells begins with the need to be grateful for feeling his blood run, his eyes blink, his muscles twitch, for having lived—a need to say "thanks for the nice time." Our life, which we did not produce, which happened through our parents though they did not fabricate it and is something the universe did not need, exists gratuitously. It was just given. Gratitude means recognizing the gift as a gift. When someone gives us a gift, we receive it with embracing hands, retain it, and provide space for it on the festive table or on the mantelpiece over the hearth fire. Because words do embrace content, because they do hold together and persist, the words "thanks for the nice time" do not simply express gratitude, exteriorize a gratitude that is inward and mental; they enact gratitude, they realize gratitude.

We can even say thanks for our ailments:

> He wants the body to be an affable host to its deadly diseases. He wants them to have a welcome, a space to move around in and show their stuff. . . . His ailments he regards as gifts given, trophies singled out to gift him with, and he takes a certain pride in owning them, in their ownership of him.[6]

"Thanks for the nice time" in the world—not because the world is such a nice place, but the world does have so many beauties that arrive gratuitously. Though we do have to contrive to see them:

> Do we embrace thoughtlessly, or do we somehow come to terms with the measured putrefaction we contain, and so develop a more open-minded sense of beauty? Severable beauty is a precarious thing, but that doesn't mean I'm duty-bound to kiss my sweetheart's feet because, properly reviewed, they're just as lovely as her lips. They're blessed, though. They help. They have structure. They call up certain Cézannes. Then

why do I carry a snapshot of her face and not of them? Am I—are we—
altogether too selective? If we relish life as such, shouldn't we admire
it in the round? We cannot make a tree. We cannot make a liver either.
And, if we could, would we take the same esthetic pride in the liver as in
the tree?[7]

Could we come to admire the world in the round by just silent contemplation? Nietzsche asked:

How can we make things beautiful, attractive, and desirable for us when
they are not? Here we could learn something . . . from artists who are
really continually trying to bring off such inventions and feats. Moving
away from things until there is a good deal that one no longer sees
and there is much that our eye has to add if we are still to see them at
all; or seeing things around a corner and as cut out and framed; or to
place them so that they partially conceal each other and grant us only
glimpses of architectural perspectives; or looking at them through tinted
glass or in the light of the sunset; or giving them a surface and skin that
is not fully transparent—all this we should learn from artists.[8]

Photographers show us beauty in the measured putrefaction that the
world about us contains and that we contain; they photograph it from a
distance where the eye has to add much, they frame it with other things
or show it partially concealed or aflame with rare lighting, or they light
up surface grain and glows. Words, just because they fragment things
and grasp them with their outlines or skeletons only or focus our attention on some unnoticed detail or some relationship with remote things,
can cast over things strange auras and spells. Perhaps indeed we can find
our sweetheart's feet beautiful just by gazing upon them in the right setting and light. Yet is it not those words—"They're blessed, though. They
help. They have structure. They call up certain Cézannes"—that give our
contemplation that boost that makes us admire them in the round of
things?

With words we move lightly over things. And words, with their
streaming and their syncopation, their soft or hard, warm or cold tonalities, their beat and their micromelodies, their rumble and their hisses,
their harmonies and their dissonances, pick up and amplify the sonorities
loud and latent in the things. In doing so, they embrace and consecrate
things and events. "Have not names and sounds been given to things
that man might find things refreshing?" Zarathustra noted. "Speaking
is a beautiful folly: with that man dances over all things. How lovely is all
talking, and all the deception of sounds! With sounds our love dances on
many-hued rainbows."[9]

And words, like the moaning with which the inner melodies of the body seek to come together again, can soothe and heal us. They can resonate through the body and help it reestablish its inner rhythms and melodies, its musicality.

The words that are bound to wounds also can break free of them; words can be an escape from illness, themselves become a life, a life of words. West discovers that the medical profession had fashioned a justifiable and concise taxonomy, which he learned not only for its utility for himself or for the old pleasures of scholarship but for the pleasure he finds in it: "I do get a sense of unique and ravishing complexity such as I get from a work of art, whether as maker or appreciator."[10] But he also escapes into writing fiction: "I keep managing to come to the end of another chapter, say, and I marvel at the plenary gratitude the human spirit can feel after the Furies have had it by the short hairs and it has managed to slink away, back into the operating theater of words."[11] So also with us: with our visitors in the hospital, how compulsively we talk of other things, leaving our illness behind. With words we connect with the words of others and with their lives. There is this ecstatic power in words.

Part 6

Recognizing Others, Contacting You

14

Recognition

In philosophy since Plato, "recognition" has been restricted to designate a cognitive operation by which a particular entity or event is subsumed under a category. Recognition would require a cognitive distance taken from that with which we find ourselves in contact. And, since Plato, philosophers have analyzed recognition in the operation of language. Yet a perceptual recognition precedes and makes possible the recognition formulated in language. Extensive biological research has now shown that other species from pigeons to primates recognize what they perceive with a categorical intelligence.[1]

There is also a recognition that does not involve taking a distance but occurs in an attraction to what is recognized. Coral fish, butterflies and wasps, birds of paradise and hummingbirds, zebras and foxes bear surface colors and patterns and utter distinctive cries with which they both recognize one another and are drawn to one another. Among us, greetings do not function through their cognitive meaning; in greeting someone, we at the same time recognize and also approach that person.

Elaborate and fantastic courtship behaviors have been much documented among jewelfish, whitefish, sticklebacks, cichlids, and guppies; among fruit flies, fireflies, cockroaches, and spiders; among crabs; among mountain sheep, antelope, elk, lions, and sea lions; and among emperor penguins, ostriches, pheasants, and hummingbirds. Not only the males but sometimes also the females adorned with fantastic colors perform the rituals of courtship.[2] The rapt attention they elicit draws the courted to the courting one.

Among humans too, the recognition by category that involves taking a cognitive distance from one another is preceded and made possible by a recognition that is simultaneously attraction to those of our kind.

The things we see; the rustle, crackling, and songs we hearken to; the roughness and the sleekness we touch are not just pieces of a puzzle we have to understand. In fact, there are no intelligible concepts that grasp the languorous liquidity of the water in the bath, the tang of lemonade, the brisk radiance of the sunshine, the velvety green of springtime, the foolishness of a kitten rolling a ball on the sidewalk and tumbling over itself. Laughter is released by the outbreak of incoherence in discourse, by slippages and collapses in our operations, and by projects that are blown off by the first wind. Surprise is the active pleasure that holds on to the giddy piece of time that just lost the support of its past and jumped the rails of the future. Our energies ricochet in peals of laughter over the naked and smug presence of things going their own way or not caring where or if they are going.

Displeasure is our weak, passive reaction to the loss or absence of things we had counted on. The strong active engagement with things decaying and dying, with a lamb hit by a passing truck and deer fleeing a forest fire, is active grief and tears, offering them our impotent support, harboring them in our heart after they are gone.

Laughter and tears make us transparent to one another. In a foreign airport the language of passengers I do not understand makes them strangers to me. A designer-dressed matron comes stalking about giving orders—then Whap! suddenly slips on the polished floor, and her voice stops with the thump of her ass. My laughter rebounds in the laughter of the others around me and theirs in mine, and I understand their laughter and understand them and understand they are people of my kind.

Coming upon a woman sitting on a park bench weeping, we do not know what loss she has suffered, but her misery is transparent to us and invades us. When a child emaciated with AIDS is wandering about lost, we see his distress through our tears.

Laughter and tears, blessing and cursing, are the fundamental forms of communication. We gather together to tell our hilarity or our sorrow; we speak of the things we bless and those we curse. Greetings, hailing or confirming whatever our interlocutor is doing or saying, and jokes, teasing, and banter—much of the talk that goes on among us does not aim at truth but at smiles and laughter. Expletives, imprecations, execrations, as also exclamations, sighs, moans, and so many questions and redundancies do not contribute information but affirm our concern for one another's afflictions and worries. Transmission of information and giving orders are secondary, sporadic forms of our speech.

As we pass by fellow humans, an undercurrent of erotic fever attaches to those like ourselves and those unlike—of a different gender or age, strangers come from afar. In a cabaret in Bangkok where a transvestite is flaunting her body, in an old folks' home where an old man is ardently caressing the face of an old woman, in a street in Hammerfest, that northernmost town of Europe, where adolescents are reveling in their nakedness in the public fountain, we glance at those beside us and their glances meet ours, and though we do not speak, perhaps do not know one another's language, we understand one another, are transparent to one another. With our erotic excitement we recognize theirs and are drawn to them. In men and women whose language and culture are alien to us and who live in regions uninhabitable by us, even in those who are most set up against us—the riot policemen mutely blocking the way of our demonstration—we divine a subtext of erotic posturing and parading, understand one another and are drawn to one another.

Human infants laugh and weep before they can speak, and they laugh and weep with one another's laughter and tears. Human infants, and now biologists,[3] recognize that chimpanzees, prairie dogs, and rats laugh. The distinctive colors, patterns, and cries that individuals recognize and that are attractive to others of their kind may also attract individuals of another species. Golden pheasants join flocks and courtship circles of Lady Amherst pheasants; buffalo have mated with yaks, lions with tigers, bottlenose dolphins with false killer whales. In their dealing with both other species in nature and domesticated species, humans have always felt confident that they can recognize their pleasures and distresses over losses; we also recognize and are attracted by the ornamentation and seductive games of other species.[4] We adorn ourselves with plumes, furs, tusks, shells, flowers; the courtship dances of cranes, bustards, and ruffs taken up in Japan, the Middle East, and Africa still shape the new fashions of our courting.

15

Contact

Every day I realize that others looking at me and talking about me or to me are only addressing some role I occupy in a society, some work I am performing, the white collar, overalls, or tank top I am wearing: they see and address the office worker, the farmer, the beach bum. While I—this individual me—think for myself and act on my own, behind that image they see. Doesn't it work the other way too? The agent or agency inside my head listening and interpreting is decoding according to its own code. So we are insistently told that we have to be made to recognize this and examine that code, its ethnic, class, race, and gender categories and paradigms. When someone there is standing before us, speaking directly to us, don't we have to take into account how this is the male or the female point of view, the urban or nomadic perspective, the way corporate officials or black prisoners see things, the way our cronies, out of so many shared interests and amusements, or the way Jamaicans or Thais in the tourist or the sex industry talk to people like us?

Yet it happens every day that someone exterior to me approaches and makes contact with *me*. "Hey you!" "Hey Al!" In the diffuse hubbub of the environment, how I feel these words coming straight at me! They have penetrated right through the garb, the pantomime, the role, and found me. The appeal they make singles out the real me, whatever I can take to be me; the demand they make is put on me. Each time I do answer on my own, I have found it undeniable that that is what has happened. I may well sense immediately that he who stands before me and addresses me has a mistaken idea of what I am and what I have done, but how his word "you" touches the real me to arise behind that mistaken idea!

When someone with whom I have been in touch only by telephone for a long time greets me, "Hey Al! Come in! How happy I am to see you!" I feel, I know that I—the real me, this individual—am welcomed. When I am insulted, the words and the gestures touch me inwardly: I can brush them off, ignore them, dismiss them with contempt, act as though my status and my composure are utterly unaffected, but inwardly I am humiliated, wounded, diminished, mortified. When someone apologizes to me for some tactless or slighting words, for some hurt or outrage, the words penetrate right to the core of my life, which is vindicated, reinstated, restored. When someone is speechless at the sight of me, visibly constrained, paralyzed, I know that he or she does feel my pain, is afflicted with my suffering. When someone, exasperated by the officious person-age, the decent and public identity with which I persist in confronting him or her, seeks deviously or directly, viciously, to hurt me, torment me, it is not that personage or my corporeal shell but me with which he or she makes contact.

16

You

To make contact with you whose physical body I see is not to grasp your identity conceptually and respect your boundaries and inner space. It is first by the tone of voice that we make contact. I catch on to your excited or bored, complicit or aggressive tone; your voice modulates my own. Greeting you with "Hey man!" the cocky tone of those words hail the man you are for yourself, committed to manly deeds—not an official, a waiter, or a stranger. To answer the engaging or dismayed tone with which someone addresses me with the measured tone of a controlled and self-contained life is, before I refuse to understand really what she will tell me, to refuse her tone—to refuse her.

"For my part, I think . . . ," you say. "I will do it." Beneath the "I" that simply designates the one now putting forth the utterance is "I am a mother," "I am a dancer," "I am an adventurer," that secret and solitary word you have put on yourself. When I address you, I do have a sense of the inner resonance and force of that word.

In the tone with which she says "Don't worry, I'll be there," I sense the caregiver the nurse is for herself, has committed herself to be. In his jeans and plaid shirt, his mud-caked work shoes, his bared arms and bronzed face, in his awkward, uningratiating way of speaking, I sense that this youth who has come to apply for my construction job is really a builder, a man committed to work with his hands on stone, cement, and wood. I went to this camp of biologists in Peruvian Amazonia that accepts paid visitors to supplement their resources, and as soon as I see her, a thirty-five-ish woman with uncombed blond hair and rough hands, greeting me in her California accent, I know she is for herself an outdoorswoman, a rain forest dweller.

To turn to someone who says, "For my part, I think . . . ," "I am not going to . . ." is to honor someone who is as good as her word. Men or women of honor will not tolerate insult; they will stand with their body, their life against anyone who impugns their honor. It is with her body on the dance floor that the dancer will answer the sneers of critics. With his body in the rioting slums, and not with arguments in the clubs and salons, the doctor answers the insults of racists. But she and he disdain to answer those who do not stand in their words.

He whom I address also can disconnect himself from his "I"—from his "I think . . . ," "I am telling you . . ."—as I can, when speaking with him, disconnect myself from what I am saying. My interlocutor can be insincere, as I can be, can dissimulate, can lie. It is she who stands in her words when she says, "Let me tell you . . ." that I will answer when she questions the me who says "I will go"; it is he who is a dancer whose demands on the dancer I say I am that I will recognize; it is he who has never sold out—Che Guevara at forty, Nelson Mandela at eighty—and who contests the youth I say I still am that I know I have to answer.

I also sometimes know that you have abandoned the word you planted in yourself in your youth to take on a purely social and successful existence. "He was soon to be head clerk; it was time to settle down," Gustave Flaubert writes. "So he gave up his flute, exalted sentiments, and poetry; for every bourgeois in the flush of his youth, were it but for a day, a moment, has believed himself capable of immense passions, of lofty enterprises. The most mediocre libertine has dreamed of sultanas; every notary bears within him the debris of a poet."[1] But then there is a visionary in every strong and healthy person, in the youth, that is, the insolence, impetuousness, brashness, and bravado of that person.

In my hypocritical or aggressive insistence to address an official identity I nevertheless do divine who you are for yourself. I speak to you as the dean, colleague, and facilitator you officially are, while in the officious tone with which you repeat the details of the university regulations I hear the control freak you are, lording it over other adults. At the zoo I defer to your role as the parent, though in the flat warnings and admonitions that I hear you addressing to your children I understand you have married and become a parent in order to pursue your inner tyrant and sadist identity. I persist in addressing you as the convenience store clerk I and the company require, though in the bored and flippant tone with which you answer my question I realize that you are a prince of the inner-city night.

For me to make contact with you is to make contact with that visionary space in which, around the word of honor you have implanted in yourself, you turn the kaleidoscope of images and omens of good and bad luck. But is such a thing possible? Is not your mind a private theater with but one possible spectator, is not your fantasy space the place where you elaborate your private myth? Of course it is possible; nothing so much fills our time together.

The old woman living alone tells of the kittens her old cat, out carousing with a disreputable alley cat, astonishingly still able to get pregnant, will have; she tells of the son in California who never writes or calls but, she knows, will visit soon; she tells of her mother who visits her sometimes, at night. It is not through the official and intelligible categories—

female, widowed, old, born in Oklahoma—that I make contact with her but in listening to her tell her stories, making contact, through laughter and tears, with her visionary space. I do so not out of some strategy to gain her recognition of who I am, nor to understand her or understand life. There is no moral to her story; I learn nothing from it, spending the time unprofitably.[2]

To respect you is to recognize and acknowledge the one you are, the one you affirm yourself to be.[3] In practice to respect a child, a foreigner, a street person, a delinquent is to listen to him or her tell his or her story.[4] For the teacher or counselor, respect is to listen to the story the troubled child in school tells; for the couple, it is to listen to the story the spouse has to tell of the dispute they fell into; for the marriage counselor, to listen to the story each of the spouses has to tell; for the psychotherapist to listen to the story the neurotic has to tell in his or her own words. To begin to respect our adversary in a dispute, our neighbor or our spouse who has become our adversary, is to listen to the way the other recounts the sequence of events that led us into this conflict.

"Everybody's got a story," the cop says with a disabused shrug, meaning that the story is put together as an alibi or a justification. And it is true that the stories he hears are extracted by the face of someone who accuses and judges. But people recounting a trip to a far-off place, grandparents emigrated long ago from another land, friends recounting events from a childhood so distant now tell stories that convey no instruction or moral and elicit neither praise nor blame. All those friends and acquaintances seated together over meals, talking on the telephone, strolling in the park, spending evenings and weekends together, making stories out of small alterations of the workplace routine, out of people encountered and things seen on walks down the sidewalk, out of spectator sports watched passively on television—everybody's got a story, and listening to the stories silences the moralizing prig within.

There are two constructions put on the stories of our experiences we first tell ourselves that must be rejected. One is the Hegelian notion that what is at stake, in these stories, in all human encounters, is the demand for recognition. Hegel bases that on his idea that there is no immediate self-consciousness; the only way I can become aware of myself is on an exterior mirror. The master sees his mastery on the prostate bodies and fearful eyes of the slave; the slave sees his servitude in the fearful force of the master. For Hegel everything we do—dress up or dress down, join a health club, go to college, have a wedding—are so many maneuvers and stratagems of our fundamental desire for recognition. But that is not the dance floor, the Mexican market, the dive boat, the rain forest, the seats in the back garden where you and I come upon each other; it is the world of politicians, where each would be nothing but for the PR they ceaselessly put out, the world of celebrities for whom even bad publicity is good publicity, for they are nothing without press agents and paparazzi. Hegel quite ignores the sense of your identity you find in the word of honor that you secretly and inwardly implant on yourself. Hegel recognizes only fear as what circumscribes our isolation and our identity; he ignores the inner joy and pride and the inward sense of surging force, the exhilaration you know in affirming, alone and to yourself, I am a sensualist, I am a runner, I am a birdman.

There is also the notion that each of us is subjected to a fundamental ethical demand that we justify our lives. This notion, that we must live our lives under accusation, an accusation in everyone who faces us, is to be resolutely refused. The story that you have to tell, to yourself and to me, is not a story of so many plans, initiatives, achievements that would be the diagram of your life. In fact, you were born by chance, and all the decisive turns in your life—that you were born in a suburb in the richest country of the world or in a hovel in the vast outer zone, that you had a normal human body or a genetic defect, that you had the brains to get through school and perhaps the university, that you happened to meet someone you fell in love with, that you are of an expansive happy disposition or melancholic, that you somehow were free to release your superabundant energies or were constricted fearfully to your needs and wants—all that was each time a matter of good or bad luck. This repeated sense of blows of good or bad luck leaves you gaping open to an outside where unintelligible, visibly random forces hold sway. Your visionary space is not an inner representation, which you contemplate and figure out, find the meaning of, understand. It is the reflections, halos, mirages of the world in which you lead your lucky and unlucky life that make you laugh and make you weep, make you cry out blessings or curses.

What imposes respect is my sense of you as a being affirming yourself in your laughter and tears, your blessings and cursings. The jeers of strikers before the threats of the factory owner, the grief of a widow—it is bravery and strength that grieves—the affection of a child for a puppy command our respect. The misery of the trapped jaguar, the exultation of the young eagle taking to flight, the playfulness of the wolf cubs command our respect.

To approach you with respect is to expose my seriousness of purpose to the flash fires of your laughter, expose my cheerfulness to the darkness of your grief, let you put your blessing on my discomfiture and suffering, expose myself to the shock waves of your curses. It is to expose myself to you—expose myself to being violated, outraged, wounded by you.

Strong Bonds

We act on the basis of our beliefs, "trusting" them, as we say, because we have reasons to believe they are true or probably true. The reasons arise from networks of knowledge in which we generally have confidence. Suspicion arises out of reasons to doubt. We doubt that what we see is really there—that what moved sinuously in the shadows of the library stacks is a serpent, that there is a puddle of water on the desert road ahead—because, looking more closely, we see the shadows of the trees on the floor; because, driving on ahead, what looked like a shimmering puddle of water vanished in the solid surface of the asphalt. We doubt what we saw because, looking more broadly, we take what we now see to be real.

We recognize that our senses sometimes deceive us; could it be that our senses are organically deceptive? Could it be that we are always dreaming, that a fabricating imagination generates what we think we really perceive or that an Evil Genius does so? We could doubt everything we perceive only if we had cause to take the abstract scientific representation, or mathematics, or a divine or demonic world behind the scenes to be more real—but they are all derived from what we perceive. Trust in our basic mental capacities and our capacities to move and act effectively precedes and makes possible our beliefs and our doubts.

We count on the utilities officials to supply us with clean water; we rely on the postal workers to route our package to its destination once we have paid for its delivery. Our expectation about the action of the individual is based on our knowledge of how the utility company or the postal system works and how the behaviors of individuals occupying a role in them are defined. We would have to have a reason to suspect that a specific individual is not behaving as expected. What is much rehearsed in public discourse—distrust in institutions—is, when reversed, commonly called confidence in them. When people are said to lack confidence in government, corporations, the church, or the press, confidence is built up in them through ensuring that their procedures and practices fulfill their function and that the individuals who hold positions in them act as required and those who fail to do so are sanctioned.

Often we count on an individual to act in certain ways because of the value that person puts on kinship, shared circumstances, or shared religious belief. When the value placed on these things is tied up with what for the individual is his or her very identity, it becomes a strong determinant of the person's action. We rely on the person to act as the guardian of a child, fellow victim of a flood, or professed Orthodox Jew, somewhat as we rely on the bus driver or city water reservoir inspector.

Every kind of social organization for the production and distribution of goods and services, power and prestige, and knowledge is maintained by the consent of individuals to fulfill their assigned roles and by coercion—by rewards and sanctions. Emile Durkheim spoke of a "precontractual" element in all social organization: prior to the explicit consent that a multiplicity of humans may give to a distribution of specific roles, individuals—each of whom is an agent that perceives, judges, and initiates actions—establish bonds of trust among themselves. Because men and women trusted one another, they could set up a community of dwellings or consent to the distribution of roles in a productive enterprise. What first and continually installs in each of us confidence in the common discourse and the common scientific endeavor is trust in those who together determine what can count as an observation in a branch of empirical or practical knowledge, what can count as reliable and accurate language in which to report observations, and what can count as an argument and as evidence for it.

Though we speak in a broad way of "trusting" institutions, bodies of knowledge, or things,[1] the core experience of trust is trusting someone. Trust is a bond that attaches to a singular individual. We trust someone who affirms something though we do not see or cannot understand the evidence or the proof this person may have: we trust the person. Trust is our bond with someone who has bound himself to us. We trust someone to do what she says or to do what is best. We believe what the person says, we believe the action being undertaken will be for the best, because we trust the person.

It is a person's word we trust—not what we believe to be the neurological or psychological determinants of the person's behavior or the social pressures on him or her. We trust someone to help us, guide us, save us, though we and this person know that to do so is not in the person's self-interest. We know the person to be capable of being mistaken or misleading us.

The faith invoked in a religious tradition is like trust in that it is attached to a personal deity whose mind and will are unknowable but who, the devotees claim to know, is omniscient, truthful, and unfailingly benevolent. Trust differs from faith in that it is attached to someone whose words or whose movements we do not understand, whose reasons or motives we do not see, and who is capable of ignorance and incompetence, mendacity and malevolence.

Trust in someone is not simply an extension of the belief that attaches to all the things that are known about the person and takes what is unknown as though it were known. Is it not because of a long past tried and true that someone becomes a trusted adviser? All rulers understand that the more they know about their subordinates, the more these subordinates know about them and the more opportunities the subordinates have to manipulate them and use them for their own interests. Is it all that we know about the values and the peer pressure of individuals in a society that induce us to trust a stranger? But to rely on a stranger's judgment is to realize that this person can judge for his or her own advantage.

We ask, when is trust warranted? Since trust is an attachment to something that is not known, there never is a demonstration of trustworthiness. All there can be is evidence of untrustworthiness. But just as in the experimental sciences there is no crucial experiment in which a hypothesis is falsified, so there is no crucial evidence that consigns any given informant, or any ethnographic report by Margaret Mead or Edward Evan Evans-Pritchard, to the murky waters of recovered memories and fiction.

Anthropologists say that what makes their discipline different from all other kinds of social sciences is the fieldwork experience. Government officials, traders, explorers, missionaries are also in the field, and longer. Is it not the heady, intoxicating, unforgettable abandon to trust that makes the anthropologist's experience so distinctive?

Ethnographers single-mindedly set out to produce the most reliable possible report of how the people they observe live and what they think. Ethnographers' observations cannot be separated from their interviewing, for what the people observed are doing is shaped by what these people believe and feel. The credibility of ethnographers' reports is generated by trust in their informants. To be sure, ethnographers scrupulously set out to check on this trustworthiness—but they can do so only by trusting the cognitive competence and the veracity of other informants.

Every anthropologist working in the field has known times when trust emerges alone, the sole force holding one from the abysses of abandon—trust in someone as far as possible from oneself in culture, education, and age, someone with whom the anthropologist has no kinship or ethnic or national or religious bonds. Indeed, upon arriving at the field, all anthropologists recognize that their lodging, food, and very survival there will depend on trusting these indigenous strangers whose language they barely understand.

Is anything more universally distributed than trusting a stranger? Every traveler has had the daily experience of interrupting a stranger's work or preoccupations to ask for directions and not being ignored or misled. Everyone who has traveled long enough has depended for his or her life on a stranger who will never be seen again and who left before even being thanked. Upon encountering an individual outside of all institutional frameworks, all confessional allegiance, all possibility of understanding motives or even words, the invitation to—the intoxication of—trust surges.

The force that breaks with the cohesion of doubts and deliberations is a birth, a commencement. It has its own momentum and builds on itself. How we feel this force! Before these strangers whose reactions to us and motivations are so opaque to us, abruptly we fix on this individual, at random, and we feel trust, like power returned after a breakdown in the generators, flooding us with light and launching us on our way.

The doctor who finds herself trusted by me knows the surgical procedures and the precautions to attend to because she has performed this surgical operation many times, but she knows that my body is unlike any body yet opened, and there is much in its conditions, its reactions to the intervention, and the uses to which I have put it and will put it that are unknown. She knows there is much she does not know; she trusts herself to be able to deal with the unknown when it shows itself. She counts on her trust of herself more than on her knowledge. Once I put my trust in her, this trust can only generate yet more trust. The force of the trust I put in her makes her trust in herself the dominant force in her, dissipating her anxieties and vacillations.

When I have trusted my surgeon, I feel I have known her more deeply than if I had listened to her, the length of an afternoon, recounting her childhood, training, and family occupations and pastimes. What I have known is the strength of her word in which she stands.

Because I have put on myself the words "I am a dancer!" "I am the guardian of this forest!" my trust reaches out for the great teacher who gives me his word that he will teach me to become the dancer I alone can become, reaches out for the comrades and strangers who will fight fires at the risk of their lives. Trust is a bond with the word and the vision of another.

Because all our knowledge is based on multiple acts of trust, the experience of pursuing knowledge is not simply reassuring, does not make us feel comfortable and safe, but is exciting, exhilarating. Once we determine to trust someone, there flows a current of strength and lightness and a distinctive freedom. We celebrate our trust in one another in our adventures, feasting, games of glamour, courage, and skill, and in epic, song, poetry, and thought.

* * *

It takes courage to trust someone we do not know. And it takes courage for the one I trust to trust himself. Trusting someone gives me courage, and my courage makes him more trustworthy and more courageous. The courage of others in fatal diseases, shipwrecks, natural disasters, or death camps can give us courage in the face of a lost cause.

Aristotle in his *Nichomachean Ethics,* listing the virtues (*arête,* meaning excellence in fulfillment of a particular function), puts courage first. It is not simply first in a list; it is the transcendental virtue, the virtue without which the other virtues—self-control, generosity, high-mindedness, friendship, truthfulness, even wit in conversation—are not possible.[2] Friendship, magnanimity, wit in conversation shared in laughter and tears, and truthfulness exist in the contact with the you that you affirm yourself to be, with your visions, respecting you, listening to your story. My contact with you is made of trust and courage.

Part 7

What We Have to Say

What Is Known

We enter language by picking up what others say, what someone, anyone, says about the food, the furniture, the playground. We hear and repeat what others say about things and situations that we ourselves can see, what are plain truths. The talk formulates the main lines of recurrent situations in the environment. It presents the environment to the child, to the visitor, to the immigrant, as already mapped out. Any effort to formulate what is distinctive to our situation comes second.

We come back from a trip to Oregon and tell about it: "The coast out there is covered with fir and pine forests. There are gorgeous sand dunes." We are recounting the names we have been told to put on the trees there and what is said about the Northwest coast. "Looks like rain" is not really a report of a personal study of weather conditions today; we say what we have, since childhood, heard people say on days like this.

Most of what we pass on when we talk we ourselves have not seen at all—that the year 2007 is upon us, that is, in the Christian, not the Islamic or Buddhist, calendar, counted from the presumed date of the birth of Jesus, who was born in a province of the Roman empire. We transmit to others what we have been trained to say in geography class, by the tabloids, by the evangelists and psychotherapists on afternoon radio. Public opinion polls do not summarize what the public thinks about the Panama invasion or the negotiations with North Korea; they sample the public on what it has retained from what the media news analysts and sound bites from politicians have told it.

The talk does not just circulate in all directions. Speakers are not just relay points of anonymous word packets. There are directions, directives in the talk in our circle—work team, neighborhood, age group, "society," pack, or gang. With brief words the group is brought to order, the talk kept moving. Watchwords, catchphrases, cues, prompts signal what to talk about and when and how.[1] They direct the choice of words and of grammatical and rhetorical form, order the tone of voice and the rapid or measured pace of our utterances and assents. Silence, put-downs, or derisive laughter sanction deviations from the group talk.

Who decrees how we must talk about the weather, California wines, rap music, the football game, and cellular phones? These dominant voices can be identified. Someone arrives at the dorm with a fringed leather jacket painted silver from San Francisco and a pierced and studded tongue he got there one night when he was stoned. There is a moment of hesitation: the group does not quite know what to say. Then the big man in the group says: "Cool." Or he says: "Where did you get that faggoty jacket? And you pierced your tongue—Sick!" These words do not convey information to us; they instead impose what we have to say.

A scatter of words both sets up a certain order in the course of a conversation and commands the other speakers. These cues or watchwords are trenchant and brief: "Cool." "Sick." "Faggoty." To get admitted into the group, we have to catch on to a set of such words that order the way college jocks, sorority sisters, or the Trench Coat Gang talk. They are passwords. When, having mastered the language of a discipline, we get our PhD and a job, we have to catch on to what vocabulary to use when attending a department meeting to discuss changes in the curriculum, how long to take to express our opinion, what serious and affable tone of voice to use, how to glance at the department head and the other faculty members, and what kind of small talk to engage in when we run into a senior professor in the hallway.

The talk does not circulate in an anonymous, faceless multiplicity such as that invoked by Heidegger's "They," *das Man.*[2] A group, a pack, a gang, a milieu, "society," and a community are defined by the attractions and repulsions, sympathies and antipathies, alliances and duplicities, penetrations and expansions that affect sensitive and susceptible bodies coupled on to implements and to other bodies. To envision it, we should envision the passionate map of the neighborhood, the city, and the province, as novelists do. William Faulkner maps out the territory by identifying the loyalties and exclusions in families, friendships and infatuations among individuals, encroachments of newcomers, old and new hatreds, alliances and ambitious and vengeful forays. The cues and watchwords that are uttered accompany and advance movements of force in such a milieu.

The collectives are multiple and overlapping. A man will, in the course of a day, speak "as a father has to" at home; dictate as the boss to his subordinates; engage in flirtatious and childish lover's talk with his lover. In falling asleep, his sleeping mind will elaborate an oneiric discourse about things that worried him during the day or about things that still bug him from his childhood; when the telephone rings, he abruptly adopts a professional voice to speak with a business associate about the urgent matter that made him ring so late.

* * *

The talk that orders a collective work, a common defense effort, or the production and exchange of commodities in a market does not simply formulate the way things are and what has to be done; a supplementary discourse justifies what is being ordered to individuals involved in that collectivity and to those outside it. Social theorists have sought to map out the range and the consistency and coherence of the reasons elaborated to justify the collective work, defense effort, productive enterprise, or market to those within and those outside of it. Identifying this discourse as the myths of a society or social movement or as the rhetoric of a political or military policy marks the distance the analysts take from its truth; identifying it as the "ideology" of a group marks their judgment that it reflects the interests of a dominant or dominated collective.

Thorstein Veblen wrote up *The Theory of the Leisure Class;* he explained how cues, signs, watchwords, slogans, decrees, and also the body language, dress, and taste in foods, clothing, and home furnishings of the leisure class all fit together in a consistent and coherent system. Since this discourse functions both to distinguish them from the working class and to justify their leisure, it cannot be taken as a simple representation of society. It functions to mask the real operations of the leisure class within society. Hence it has to be brought to light and interpreted by the sociologist. The overall vision and the thoroughgoing cynicism of the theory of the leisure class are themselves powerful instruments of the domination exercised by that class.

Karl Marx and more recently Pierre Bourdieu wrote up the theory of the working class. Neither has written up the theory of inner-city street people, whom Marx set aside as lumpen proletariat, unreliable in the worker's movement. Their ideas were taken to be naive: they are in fact mystified by the ruling class. Oscar Lewis saw this gap in our understanding of what he called the "culture of poverty." He set out, during long years spent in the slums of Mexico City, to discover and write up the worldview of the extremely poor. But his project came apart by itself: what he wrote was *The Children of Sanchez,*[3] in fact the biographies of the various members of a single family and what they said in their own words.

The lumpen proletariat, the inner-city poor, the slum dwellers do not form a homogeneous class, but instead milieus, clans, marginals, packs, and gangs linked by attractions and repulsions, sympathies and antipathies, alliances, and penetrations where individuals are coupled on to a few implements and a few luxury objects and to other individuals. Cues, watchwords, passwords order these couplings. They are discontinuous utterances. They are not derived from a coherent ideology.

Is not that also true of the leisure class and the dominant classes of history? The concept of ideology attributes an overall unity and an improbable intelligence and cynicism to a society or social movement, political or military policy, or dominant class. In fact, the beliefs people have about their interests can well be rationalizations of wishful thinking or excessive pessimism. The beliefs that people in a social position or a ruling or dominant group have may not serve their interests. Beliefs that do serve certain interests are not necessarily to be explained by those interests.

Michel Foucault showed that the procedures of surveillance, control, and discipline of the modern institutional archipelago were invented piecemeal. Once mechanisms of social power are invented, they can be used in diverse ways, one of which is dominance.[4] The cues and watchwords that order these uses also are invented piecemeal. What makes language powerful, a language of power, is not the consistency and coherence of an overall theory of domination—which the social critique in fact does not unearth but constructs—but the peculiar force of fragmentary, discontinuous, order words in local power couplings.

Collective work and common defense require language that formulates truly the way things are and what has to be done. Reliable judgments and informed commitments make the market work. Group adventures and follies require some real knowledge.

The terms of working language are categories; they record the recognizable features of an entity or an event—features that recur as the moments pass, in this entity or event as in others like it. They record what is recognizable by others. To formulate an entity or event truthfully is to situate oneself in a series of observers and truth tellers.

Rational knowledge consists of statements for which reasons are or can be given. Rational reasons invoke empirical evidence or necessary consequence from other established statements—which are available to anyone with insight. The practice of giving and demanding reasons submits every rational statement to question, to criticism, or to acceptance by just anyone with insight and understanding. Someone who speaks rationally admits anyone endowed with insight as the judge of what he or she says. This practice invokes a potential rational community.

The rational community subdivides into various scientific and technological communities. Communication within a scientific discipline or among workers in a technological field is based on determinations of what could count as observations, what standards of accuracy in determining observations are possible, how the words of common language are restricted and refined for formulating observations in various scientific disciplines and practical or technological uses. Further, there are determinations of what could count as an argument—in logic, in physics, in history, in literary criticism or biblical scholarship, in economics, in penology, jurisprudence, and military strategy, or in medical treatment.

In scientific and technological work, the decisions as to what counts as an observation and as an argument are made by experts. The authorities do not validate their decisions by a structure of reasons found outside the science or the practice. Instead, they consider what taxonomy has been in use in the science so far and what standards of accuracy in determining observations have been maintained until now. When they decree that new terms marking discriminations or new standards of accuracy should be introduced, their expertise is validated by the acceptance and practice of the specific scientific or technological community.

Scientific or technological work requires institutions that set up and finance research teams and laboratories to gather data according to professional standards of accuracy and repeatability as well as institutions that select and train researchers and technicians. Establishing what can and must be said about things requires institutions that select what research is to be published and how it is to be judged.

In a scientific research team, the talk is not determined simply by the importance of the topic and the intrinsic sequence of problems to be solved. It also is ordered by the enthusiasms and obsessions, professional and financial ambitions, and envies of someone who emerges as leader, issuing watchwords, prompts, and slogans.[5]

In living and working in an environment of natural resources, industry, markets, and collective defense, we work with a common stock of formulations taken as "what is known." While a good deal of it may be unreliable observations, guesswork, and hearsay disseminated by the media held to deadlines and the need to dramatize, much of it consists of plain truths.[6] The seventeenth-century apologists for empirical science characterized what was taken as known by prior ages as inextricably riddled with myth and superstition and buttressed with the specious authority of ancestors or gods. Anthropologists today recognize that no society that survived over time could have done so unless its knowledge of its environment was fundamentally sound.

The common knowledge that a society possesses is the basis for the elaboration of rational knowledge. Geology begins with the common knowledge about mountains and jungles, rivers and ocean shores formulated in the course of the inhabitation, migrations, journeys, and settlements of humans. Biology, botany, pharmacology, and astronomy presuppose the common knowledge that first identified and located other animals, vegetables, minerals, and celestial bodies. The mathematical calculations with which the anthropologist Claude Lévi-Strauss represents the elementary and composite relations of kinship in gender-based societies presuppose alliances and recognitions of descent with which those societies form, and with which individuals associate without having calculated their forms of association mathematically, and interact with the anthropologist who comes to them. Scientific objectivity that requires that every observation be repeatable and verifiable by others, by just anyone—with the proper equipment for observation, the vocabulary, and the training in the reasonings canonical in this empirical domain—appears as a refinement of the commonness of common knowledge. Technological operations still and always require the common knowledge of body maneuvers and skills of individuals who leave their beds and their homes for laboratories and factories. Common knowledge still locates for scientific researchers their laboratories, their implements, and their books.

As observations and generalizations established in the theoretical and technological sciences pass into the usage of laboratory workers and engineers and are disseminated in textbooks used in schools and by media news reports and features, they enlarge the body of what a society takes as common knowledge. They are added to the stock of what is taken as known by artisans and skilled workers, people competent in social relations, ancestors and religious leaders, as well as people who simply are engaged in the life of this city or this land. Over time some kinds of statements predominate, others are less and less appealed to or presupposed; conflicting statements may be rephrased to soften or eliminate the conflict.

Specialized discourses are but partially embodied in the discourse of any representative speaker; anthropologists will not find all the myths or religious dogmas of a culture in any informant, not in even the religious experts of that culture. People who rely on what is taken to be commonly known remain open to correction by the better informed.

Observation reports and the formulation of regular relationships between entities and events originally formulated insights. When they are repeated as part of "what is known," their repetition does not function to reanimate or even recall the insights they originally formulated. Now, their function is practical; they figure not as depictions of an observed situation but as orders being issued. They select areas for new observations and order new classifications and formulations of regularities in nature and in economic or social behavior. They organize and order the planning and execution of practical activities. They function not as theoretical hypotheses but as group imperatives.

They function with collectives, connected by sympathies and antipathies, alliances and jealousies, devoted to enrichment through the exploitation of resources, labor sources, and markets; to collective defense; or to colonial, imperial, or corporate expansion. They direct movements of people seeking attachments and alliances with families, clans, other cultures, destitute peoples, with historical achievements and with landscapes and ecosystems. They animate gatherings and schisms within "society" and launch milieus, gangs, packs into adventures and follies.

19

When I Have to Speak

The established rational discourse of the sciences and technologies not only organizes the regions of observed nature, implements, societies, and histories with its empirical laws supplying reasons for observations and its theories supplying reasons for empirical laws, but it also orders the discourse of individuals. The rational discourse of the sciences and technologies depends on speakers whose utterances formulate insights that can only be the insights of real individuals, who undertake to answer for what they say, to supply evidence for its truth.

Individuals are ordered to formulate what they see and experience in the established concepts of the language and in forms that can be verified. What they see and experience is divested of the individual light and tone they have for the one who sees and experiences them, and divested of the surprise and the significance they had when that person came upon them. Then an individual speaks as someone in whose statements are implicated the logic, theories, and cognitive methods of the rational community; he or she speaks as a representative, equivalent to and interchangeable with others, of the established truth. She speaks as a veterinarian, an electrician, a computer programmer, a public health nurse. He formulates his anxiety attacks in terms of contemporary psychiatry; she names her aches and pains with the terminology of scientific medicine. An individual's very body sees and feels as an ophthalmologist, a ferryboat captain, a lab technician, a British or Hong Kong subject. How many people we see whose bodies we cannot imagine without military uniform or fatigues, gray flannel suit or tennis shirt and shorts, professor's tweeds or farmer's jeans!

In the course of our education, learning language and learning the languages of various disciplines, there are periodic examinations to verify whether we have mastered the authorities of the discipline. Then the professor calls upon the student: "But what do you think?" "Write an essay." The sociology, modern languages, or philosophy professor herself will be expected to periodically give papers at conferences, displaying her expertise of the field, her mastery of the canonical authorities, but a senior professor is expected to put forth some thesis or judgment in her own name. The veterinarian normally speaks as a representative of the current state of veterinary science, but from time to time the client demands he formulate his own judgment. His judgment will be critically appraised, perhaps by another veterinarian called upon to give a second opinion. If the judgment followed turns out to result in extreme pain, crippling, or death, he may be charged in a malpractice suit. The right and the duty to speak in one's own name is established by the rational collective.

Every collective requires that what it takes as known be essentially sound, and thus it also requires individuals who formulate their insights into the situation and possibilities before them and answer for their formulations. The circulation of traffic and the banking system require citizens to report malfunctionings and contribute insights for improvement. Clubs and public beaches require individual insights into changing norms of propriety. To be recognized as members of a gang, a subcult, a team, a neighborhood, or a profession, individuals find themselves ordered to speak. The group requires the individual's insights and requires that they be formulated in the vocabulary and grammar of the common language.

The right to speak in our own name gives us space to exist, a space furnished with equipment and opportunities. The duty to speak in our own name is imposed under threat of exclusion or effacement from the practicable space of the discipline, technological team, "society," the milieu, pack, or gang. In finding ourselves ordered to speak in our own name, we find ourselves being circumscribed, called to account, the space of our impassioned experiences annexed to the group. The order, prompt, or cue that orders us to speak in our own name is already, Deleuze and Guattari say, a verdict, a death sentence.[1] Abrasive words, stinging words, biting words, cutting words order us. Death is not only a limit, an end, in time; it is also a limit in space. Every prompt and password limits the space in which we live. The collective sows words that constrict us, lacerate us, humiliate us, sicken us, mortify us.

20

What I Have to Say to Myself

I can see and report on the front of my body from my chest down, and with a mirror I can observe my face, my back, my stance and movements. I can note physical pains, itches, pressures, heat and cold. I can recall and report on actions I have undertaken, events that surprised me, moods that came over me, pleasures I have felt, thoughts and intentions I have had, decisions I have taken. These observations and memories can be partial, fleeting, superficial, erroneous, and corrected. There is also much that I can observe only with the aid of complex technology (the processes of digestion, the enervation of muscle systems) or cannot observe (the integration of sensations and the processing of information).

Being awake contains a sense of existing and existing here and now. As I stand, walk, sit, or open doors and handle implements, I have an awareness of the axis and orientation of my posture. As I read, I have a sense of the position of my legs under the table; as I climb a ladder, I have a sense of the position of my legs and hands without looking at them. As I make my way through a crowd or through the narrow turns of a cave, I have a sense of the volume my body is occupying. This awareness is not the result of observation; it is internal to my body's positions and movements and produced by taking up the positions and enacting the movements. In the measure that I relax completely and let my arms and legs settle by gravity, my sense of their extension and positions fades out. I also have a sense of where I am in time without looking at outer markers of time: I have a sense of where I am in the morning sequence of awakening, going to the toilet, shaving, dressing, and making breakfast. During a hike I am aware that I have been walking only a short time or a long time already.

There is a consciousness of my emotions, desires, beliefs, and decisions that is intrinsic to them. It shapes them, in the way that playing the piano unreflectively, attentively, or deliberately to annoy someone makes for different ways of playing the piano. I can be ill at ease and agitated while my attention is wholly focused on a mathematical or mechanical problem that I am trying to work out. In becoming aware of a state of malaise, feeling resentment or impatience, I become aware of a situation in which I am involved: I have been passed over and denigrated by my superior, or a former lover has telephoned that she will be arriving at five o'clock. Becoming aware of the state of malaise or impatience includes the disdainful superior or the arriving ex-lover emerging in relief before me, and it includes my attention turned to the one or the other with recoil or with anticipation. Becoming conscious of the disdainful superior and of my resentment of him may bring into sharper relief the condescending comportment of the superior and focus and intensify my resentment, or it may motivate an effort to turn away from him and neutralize the emotion I feel. If I formulate what I feel, doing so also will affect the subsequent evolution of my emotion: if I think that my feeling of gratitude is bound up with resentment and aggression toward my benefactor or is a kind of shameful neurotic dependence, these thoughts will affect how I behave toward my benefactor. The consciousness is not a distant observation of the emotion; it is internal to the emotion, endorsing it.

Similarly the consciousness of my beliefs and decisions is an intrinsic quality in them. So many, indeed most, of my beliefs, taking as true so many things that have been perceived or that I have read about, are implicit or unconscious. They are embedded in a vast array of inference patterns, conceptual commitments, and dispositions to behave. When beliefs and decisions become explicitly conscious, they are no longer states that occur to me or are latent in me; they become mine. A conscious desire is a desire I endorse;[1] it is a desire for which I am responsible. It can give rise to deliberation about the reasons I can adduce for finding it realizable or unfeasible and the reasons for finding it justified pragmatically as well as morally or not so justified. The deliberation I can pursue about my desires and decisions makes it possible for me to affirm that they are rational.

Explicit consciousness of my postures and movements or of my emotions, desires, beliefs, and decisions can interrupt their continuity and interfere with their course. Attention to the positions of my fingers interferes with the typing; attention to my postures and moves disrupts the kinetic melody of the dance; attention to the succession and unfolding of my thought processes muddles the problem-solving or creative operation of thought. When there is no cause for deliberation or review of them, the explicit consciousness fades, leaving only the consciousness intrinsic to postures and movements that are occupied with tasks in the environment, and intrinsic to emotions and desires absorbed in outlying things or events. An important and urgent task can absorb our attention; an intriguing puzzle or a musical composition can hold us in thrall, a vast and serene vista or a vibrant sky can effect any center such that self-consciousness is dissolved in them.

* * *

I am bored with this lecture, I am going to try to make a good impression, I am hungry, this traffic is getting on my nerves, I feel stressed out, I really should not be watching this television trash. The kind of self-consciousness that is an intrinsic quality of our postures and movements and of our emotions, desires, beliefs, and decisions is rarely noted in ordinary language or in philosophical discussions of consciousness and self-consciousness. What is called "self-consciousness," being explicitly concerned with "ourselves," is especially preoccupation with our discomforts, lacks, wants, lassitude, and boredom and our intentions, appetites, and volitions. The conscious preoccupation with them endorses them and shapes them: it brings them and their correlates in the environment into relief. It can develop into a voiced or unvoiced language identifying them and specifying their urgency.

It is "the most superficial and worst part" of ourselves, Nietzsche said, that is formulated in the language of self-consciousness.[2] The inner commentary about our needs and wants formulates the self negatively as a bundle of needs and wants. But wants and needs are intermittent and superficial; the core of ourselves is positive, is the organism that generates energies in excess of what is needed to compensate for losses and maintain itself. Because it produces excess energies within itself, it has to act to discharge them in some enterprise, adventure, or play, and because it acts, it develops specific needs and wants.

It is striking that we have few, and such vague, words to speak of states of full and energetic engagement in tasks, of vibrant absorption in complexly evolving spectacles or in music, or of being immersed in warmth and light, in desert landscapes or ocean depths. As infants we needed no words for our romping animal energies and exuberances, accompanied with cries and laughter. The words we had to learn were words for our needs, our hungers, our discomforts. We learned to formulate them in the general words of public language so that others could understand them and attend to our needs and wants. Self-consciousness formulates our life for ourselves as needy and dependent. Expressing ourselves in the commonplaces of language is debilitating and capitulating.

When we engage in this language, we end by making our words true. Expressing ourselves as a bundle of needs and cravings, we make ourselves common and dependent, parasitic. We apply ourselves to acquiring commodities with which to nourish, refurbish, and protect ourselves and to fill up the space and the time. What is ephemeral, transitory, fragmentary, cryptic, or gratuitous makes us feel vulnerable.

Others do understand and want to hear about our needs and lacks. Our needs and wants are apprehended by them as appeals, expressions of dependence on them, declarations of subservience, invitations to subjugation. "You're bored? You're tired. Then come up to bed," says the mother, looking forward to an uninterrupted movie on television. Through our needs and lacks we appeal to the will in the others—the will to power in the others, the will to dominate. "You want to get out of the house—you want a motorcycle? Then go get a job."

The self-consciousness in which we deliberate about our needs, wants, appetites, intentions, and volitions is critical and guilty. It requires a meaning and a justification for them, which deliberation can never settle.

Here I am, in midlife, settled in this house, this town, this job—why am I so restless? Married and with children, I find myself obsessed with another man whom I see every day in the office. Backpacking for a year across Africa after graduation, seeing in land after land so many people barely surviving, I remember what I told my parents: that I needed to discover the world and discover myself. What sense to make of my situation, my life, of life and of death?

Is this man really in love with me? As soon as the question arises, everything he does becomes a sign to be interpreted—every phrase he uses, every sigh or gasp in lovemaking, whether he comes early or comes late, whether he dresses up or dresses down. What does it mean that I am having an affair? In trying to formulate a response to the question, I find that the terms of my response invoke other terms with which they contrast, the meaning determined in a context of meaning. If I question the meaning of any of those terms, I only find myself on another level of discourse where again the terms hold together by contrast with one another. What does infidelity really amount to? What does duty mean—duty to my children and duty to myself? I find that the circles in which marriage has meaning and in which love has meaning intersect without coinciding.

In the crowds in the streets, on the beaches, the eyes that glance at us see the sculpture of our features, the halo of our hair, the spring of our gait, the voluptuous curves of breasts and thighs. Their questions—"How goes things?" "When did you get here?" "Hey, how about this crowd!"—elicit meaningless replies, simple affirmations of togetherness, murmurings of shared pleasure. Our gaze warms with the familiarity of the face of a friend, appreciating once again those green eyes, that swath of auburn hair; we enter once again the beach games of banter and gossip, we argue once again over the mechanical problems of our motorcycles, we make bets on the race or the stock market.

Then someone, breaking with the flow and jumble of things, turns to us and asks what our new situation will mean, what our behavior is supposed to mean. His face is a screen pulled over the substance of a tanned complexion, squat nose, balding head, a screen on which forms the dark hollow of a question and a demand.[3] His eyes are not colored spheres exposed for our contemplation; they single us out, hold us and address us.

Our father turns off the video game and seats himself in front of us. Our wife looks at us in the eyes and asks what is wrong.

We look to her eyes to see if she is pleased or displeased with our response, if her eyes sanction or stigmatize. The pleasure or displeasure is not like a color or shape on them; it is the trace of the inward movement of her subjectivity. Every assent we see there is only provisional, for our response does not fix its meaning in itself and requires a clarification, explanation, justification, and every clarification an explanation in turn: the eyes that fix us are black holes.

"What've you been up to?" said as a greeting when we arrive on the beach can open upon any of several yarns or banter. "What've you been up to?" said by a mother who faces her teenage daughter who has been out all night—fixes a single line of discourse. The response must line up the multiple and equivocal movements of the night into a coherent explanation, in the terms demanded by the question. "But I love that man!" "You mean you admire his wit and savoir-faire!" "You are just grateful for all he has done for you!" "Don't you just mean you have the hots for him?" "Yes or no?"

The teacher spoke to our parents about our poor grades. Our parents wondered why in college our friends all seemed to be same sex. Our wife suggests there is a reason why we are not doing something about all the weight we are putting on. Every time we turn on the television there are those faces: pundits and senators discussing the low vote turnout, psychiatrists discussing the reasons for child molestation and sociologists discussing the reasons for the current wave of child molestation scandals, preachers demanding what it means that we don't seem to care that no real meaning can be assigned to our lives, to human life on earth. Week after week the newsmagazines analyze why there are now high-school kids shooting down their comrades in school, what it means for the baby boomers to be settling down, why people are buying more and more cellular phones. These feature articles are signed, and, across from the table of contents page, they show photos of the authors' faces.

In the back room of our self-consciousness we prepare a response to the others, we prepare admissions, excuses, and justifications. A life continually becoming explicitly self-conscious is a life lived under a shifting and generalized accusation.

Not only our mouth feels beset upon, forced to utter unending explications of every word, but also our bodies. For words energize, prod, badger, poke at, harass, excite, agitate, soothe, hypnotize, and stupefy our bodies.

21

What I Have to Imagine

While the term "myth" in the polemics of positivists and in much current discourse designates the fantasies of a collectivity, in anthropology "myth" designates a discourse, common to a community, that arises out of and gives rise to ritual. Its categories appear as archetypal images or symbols; its narrative plot represents their relationships, conflicts, combinations, and resolutions. Myths are taken to provide a meaning to the actions and inactions of individuals, the undertakings and common projects of a collective, and the lives of a human collectivity among other collectivities and among other species in nature.

It happens that two societies and two myths enter into contact— the Islam of the Arab invaders and the old Zoroastrianism of the Persians; the white mythology of priests and missionaries and the old African mythologies of enslaved peoples in Mississippi, Brazil, and Haiti. Two political systems, two economies, and also two mythologies pull in different directions in the activities and also in the understanding of people. There results not only mental confusion but physical inability to function in this field of contradictions.

In the in-between zone, where the two cultures and mythical systems imperfectly overlap, marginal leaders—medicine men, faith healers, Vodou *serviteurs*, cargo cult messiahs—work. They interpret the enslavement and deportation from Africa to Brazil, Haiti, and Mississippi in terms of the deportation and enslavement of the Jews in Egypt; they identify the triumphant white-skinned saints set up in the altars of Catholicism, Saint James and Saint George, with Ogum and Oxossi, African gods of war and knowledge. Their work is not simply to construct coherence between the universal categories of divergent myths; it is to construct coherence between the universal categories of myths and the concrete experience of individual people. They have to enable individuals to make sense of their ametropic lives.

They work piecemeal, rather like jurisprudence works. The healers and *serviteurs* operate by bricolage, by tinkering with the system, using parts of Christian mythology and parts of Aztec or Yoruba mythology to make sense of what is happening in this individual. They have to fill in the gaps; they invent, they work by inspiration. They improvise rituals and sacraments. And shamans really do, in many cases, succeed in making individuals functional again; healers really do heal.[1]

Field anthropologists found that typically shamans and healers had undergone some severe crisis in their lives. They had fallen into deep depressions, had fallen prey to strange sicknesses, had suffered physical and nervous collapse. Now they help other dysfunctional individuals by individualizing myths to explain their sicknesses and diagram cures. Are shamans and healers in fact neurotics and psychotics, improvising religions—which Freud called collective neuroses? Or should we say that neurotics and psychotics have shamans, witch doctors, Vodou *serviteurs* inside them—or that they are shamans, witch doctors, Vodou *serviteurs* occupied only with themselves? Claude Lévi-Strauss and Jacques Lacan conceived the fantasy systems of neurotics and psychotics as private myths.

But does not each of us elaborate such private myths? The common language of physical dynamics and electromagnetism, and of physiology, neurology, psychology, and pragmatic reason—the meaning system of our culture—has to be applied to our environment and our bodies in order to enable us to make sense of how our bodies function or do not function in the situations in which we find ourselves. In seeking to do so, we may find that the symbolic system has internal flaws or else that it does not adequately fit our environment. Moreover, the meaning system, the categories, are general, while we are individuals in particular situations. There is a gap; each of us has to fill in, with meaningful terms, this gap. The symbols we each devise to cover over the gap will be particular to ourself. They populate a fantasy space that is individual to each of us and which consists not simply of a floating mass of images but a personal system of interpretation.

For Immanuel Kant the rational community is the first and only form of community in which each individual practices respect for the others. What commands our respect for other people is the evidence that they exist on their own as rational agents. A rational agent is not just driven this way and that by external lures and internal unconscious drives and instincts. He or she is also not deluded by fantasies. What we respect in others is their rational faculty, that power in them to lead their own lives according to what they understand.[2] But this respect concerns not individuals in their individuality but only that faculty in them that is the same in all. Would not that individuality lie in the "private myth" each individual elaborates?[3]

It is especially with regard to what we find gives us pleasure, what elicits and stimulates our desires, what gives us a sense of satisfaction and fulfillment that the meaning system of the culture is wanting. It is especially with regard to our bodily cravings and carnal desires that we elaborate our fantasy, our private myth. Fantasy is intrinsically bound to the sensual impulses of our body. Fantasy, Slavoj Žižek says, is the particular way each of us "dreams his world," "organizes his enjoyment."[4]

Immanuel Kant argued that we have no real concept of happiness. We can give an abstract idea of it, but no thinker has been able to give the working formula. None of us who pursue happiness really knows, really can say, what this happiness is.[5] What Lacan called *jouissance,* the excessive and monstrous paroxysms of pleasure in pain, is the objective intrinsically absent from the objects of desire. It is also absent from its concept, absent from our understanding, unrepresentable.

Desire is desire for satisfaction; it can exist only as a desire that believes that it will be, or can be, satisfied. Desire persists under the illusion that in its fantasy space, it knows what it seeks and that what it seeks is obtainable. Our fundamental fantasy, then, is the way each of us conceals the irremediable absence of the object of drive. Daniel Paul Schreber's fundamental fantasy of being a slut irresistible to God projects his desire for beatitude or jouissance and covers over its impossibility.

But it is the illusionary, fragile, and helpless character of the fantasy space in the core of an individual, Žižek says, that gives an individual dignity.[6] It is what makes an individual not be content with the simple satisfaction of his or her needs and wants, not be content with contentment.

For Kant, dignity is an end that is not at the same time a means for something further. For Žižek, dignity resides in that fantasy space that makes any state of the individual be not the end but a means for a further end. It is what makes life not be simply the satisfaction of needs. This dignity, then, Žižek, like Kant, defines only negatively.

But the fantasy space in another commands our respect. Respect is attention to, considerateness for, deference to another. To respect another is to avoid violating the otherness of the other. This otherness, what Žižek calls "that part of him that we can be sure we can never share,"[7] is not an abstract separate identity but the particular fantasy that organizes his enjoyment and thus his desires and his behaviors. It is the very illusionary, fragile, and helpless character of that fantasy that requires our respect.

This conception Žižek turned into a very radical critique of psychoanalytic practice:

> But is not the very aim of the psychoanalytic process to shake the foundations of the analysand's fundamental fantasy, i.e., to bring about the "subjective destitution" by which the subject acquires a sort of distance toward his fundamental fantasy as the last support of his (symbolic)

reality? Is not the psychoanalytic process itself, then, a refined and therefore all the more cruel method of humiliation, of removing the very ground beneath the subject's feet, of forcing him to experience the utter nullity of those "divine details" around which all his enjoyment is crystallized?[8]

Psychoanalysis works to expose Schreber's conviction that he was becoming a woman with an ass irresistible to God as a mere fantasy with no basis in reality. It works to make this subject face the fact that he is in reality not a beloved child of God, that he is really the child of this father and this mother and is not a poor lost orphan, that he is a shell-shocked soldier and not a bird. Psychoanalysis is disrespect itself, the most far-reaching, deepest, and most cruel humiliation.

For us to respect the fantasy space of another, we must recognize that the meaning that we find in the world derives not simply from the common language of physical dynamics and electromagnetism, physiology, psychology, and pragmatic reason but also from our own fantasy; that the meaning that we find in our bodies and in our predicament is a private myth. To do so is to recognize that this myth functions to conceal from us the impossibility of what we desire. By acquiring some distance from our fundamental fantasy, Žižek says, we recognize the contingency of the manner in which we organize our universe of meaning and its impotence to really incorporate the other into it.[9]

Then, paradoxically, in order for the psychoanalyst, and each of us, to respect the other, we must shake the foundations of our own fundamental fantasy, force ourselves to experience the utter nullity of those "divine details" around which all our enjoyment is crystallized. Then is not the means of respecting the other a refined and cruel method of humiliation exercised on ourselves?

Žižek later repudiated this radical critique of psychoanalysis; he will instead espouse a more rigorous exposition of Lacan's interpretation of Freud.

There are positive forces in our body: the instinctual forces, limited and periodic, which integrate our body and make it functional, able to act to discharge the excess energies it produces. There is also in our body an insistent drive for excessive and monstrous paroxysms of pleasure in pain. This drive seizes hold of some organ of the body and pushes it to endlessly repeat the same failed gesture. The drive dismembers and disintegrates the organism; it is a drive toward the death of the organism, a death drive, but the drive itself knows no death and knows no time; it is a repetition compulsion. The drive is held in abeyance not by the natural integration of body parts but from the outside, by prohibition, by law.

The prohibition, this law, is imbedded in the language and symbols of the community. The explanatory systems of nonscientific cultures, as the language of our physical dynamics and electromagnetism and of physiology, neurology, psychology, and pragmatic reason, fix terms for us, each of which is a relay to further terms in the context, which opens indefinitely before our advance. The symbolic system that maps the environment for us makes action—mobilized, integrated, focused, oriented action, and action with others—possible. To channel our energies into actions is to renounce immediate gratification, to renounce the drive for excessive and monstrous paroxysms of pleasure in pain. It is to pursue the limited objectives articulated in the symbolic system, each of which is a relay toward further objectives.

Fantasy reenacts the drama of the original prohibition, the original castration. It depicts the lost object of drive as something that was taken from us by another and must be found in the other. This other is the symbolic system, but it is also he or she who utters the prohibition and subjects us to the unending pursuit of symbolized objects, symbolic objectives.

The symbolic system opens for action and for the desire that launches thought and action in innumerable and in themselves equivalent directions. Fantasies do not simply realize our desires in a hallucinatory way, thus putting an end to action and desire. Instead, they provide desire with its coordinates; they structure, channel, our desires. They constitute desire, the insatiable melancholy longing in us, Žižek says, that interminably slides from one object to another.[10]

Fantasies depict the individual as equipped and arrayed with the goods designated by the symbolic system in order to appear worthy of the desire of another, locus of the lost object of drive. Fantasies visualize what others want of me. According to Žižek, "The original question of desire is not directly 'What do I want?', but 'What do *others* want from me? What do they see in me? What am I to others?'"[11] The subject that fantasizes is at bottom a hysteric: ceaselessly questioning his or her existence, refusing to fully identify with that object others see in him or her, wondering "Am I really *that*?"[12]

> For animals, the most elementary form, the "zero form," of sexuality is copulation; whereas for humans, the "zero form" is *masturbation with fantasizing* (in this sense, for Lacan, phallic *jouissance* is masturbatory and idiotic); any contact with a "real," flesh-and-blood other, any sexual pleasure that we find in touching *another* human being, is inherently

traumatic, and can be sustained only insofar as this other enters the subject's fantasy-frame. . . . Even at the moment of the most intense bodily contact with each other, lovers are not alone, they need a minimum of phantasmic narrative as a symbolic support—that is, they can never simply "let themselves go" and immerse themselves in "that."[13]

What, then, is falling in love—what Žižek called the "mechanism, the automatism of love?"[14] We have first a fantasy of an other who would give us everything, make our existence complete. To attract that other, we depict ourselves in fantasy as worthy of a lover's total devotion; we depict ourselves equipped and arrayed with the goods depicted in the symbolic system of the culture—we identify with one of the Lotharios or sweethearts of Hollywood romances. Then abruptly someone—someone contingent, ultimately indifferent: it could be just anyone[15]—is taken to fit that fantasy frame, to materialize Mr. Right or Miss Right. To love in practice involves respect for that person who is Mr. Right or Miss Right for me—that is, respect for the fantasy Miss Right or Mr. Right that I am for him or her.

In order to be operative, fantasy has to maintain a distance from the explicit symbolic system or systems of the culture and to figure as a transgression of those systems. "'Not all is ideology, beneath the ideological mask, I am also a human person' is *the very form of ideology*, of its 'practical efficiency.' . . . *It is only the reference to such a trans-ideological kernel which makes an ideology 'workable.'*"[16] Whereas earlier Žižek had seen in the fantasy space the individuality of the individual, now the apparent individuality turns out to be but a mask that covers over the illusionary, fragile, and helpless longing for the other who would or could supply, from the outside, the lost excessive and monstrous paroxysms of pleasure in pain.

Žižek no longer depicts fantasies as utterly particular, unable to be made part of a larger, universal, symbolic medium; instead they acquire their form and force from the symbolic system. It is not simply that my imagination is too weak to create them and allows them to invade me from the outside—today from the fantasy-production machine that is the media. (We could point out that fantasies are not produced by machines; as fantasies they are produced in a psychic space, be that of the producers and directors of media dramas, infotainment programs, and marketing experts.) Rather, my fantasies acquire their form and force from the symbolic system because they answer the demands put to me by others. And Žižek's conception no longer gives rise to respect for the private myths of individuals and the practice of a specific kind of understanding of these private myths, an understanding that would presumably formulate itself

in particularizing symbols. Instead it opens upon studies of popular culture and the fantasy machinery of the mass media.

In *The Plague of Fantasies*, Žižek no longer proposes respecting the
fantasy space of individuals; instead he advocates traversing the fantasy,
letting drive break through, in its immortal repetition compulsion, which
recycles endlessly the monstrous forces of libido in an ignorance of the
limited resources and needs of the organic body. At the end of *The Ticklish
Subject*, Žižek writes, "What psychoanalytic ethics opposes to this totalitar-
ian *You may!* [the 'bad' superego version of 'You may!'] is not some basic
You mustn't!, some fundamental prohibition or limitation to be uncondi-
tionally respected (Respect the autonomy and dignity of your neighbour!
Do not encroach violently upon his/her intimate fantasy space!)." Instead
"Lacan's maxim 'Do not compromise your desire!' fully endorses the
pragmatic paradox of ordering you to be free: it exhorts you to dare."[17]

Fantasy sustains an unending openness, sustains the notion that
there is some radical Otherness that makes our universe incomplete. Traversing the fantasy, Žižek says, involves acceptance of a radical ontological
closure. We will have ceded the unending horizons extended by fantasy.

Part 8

My Own Voice

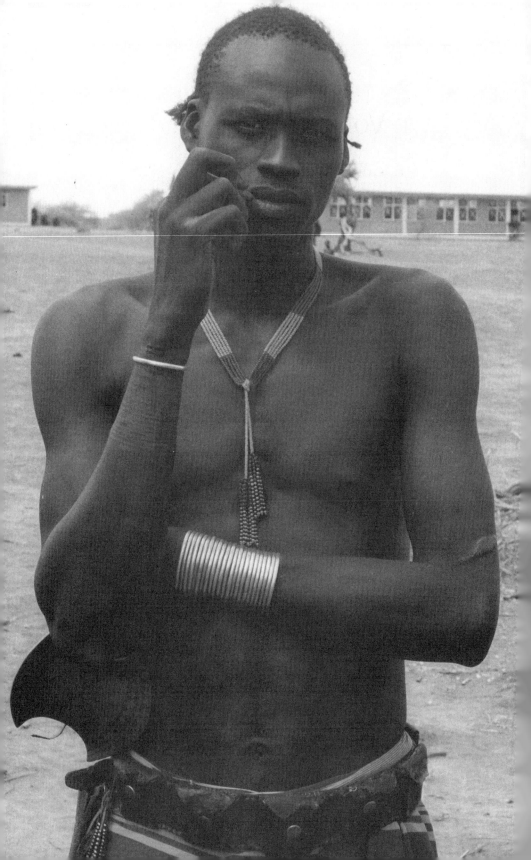

Finding Our Own Voice

A myth is not simply the particular way a particular community organizes the environment into a meaningful pattern. It is not simply a map of the environment using more concrete symbols than those used in modern economics, sociology, political science, history, biology, physics, and astronomy. Myths are also visions, visions of visionaries and seers. Visions are not just overarching conceptual frameworks; they are visualizations. The visions of Dante, William Blake, and James Joyce, those of the *Epic of Gilgamesh* and the *Mahabharata,* the *Iliad* and the *Ring of the Niebelung* present a transfigured and glorified world or the glowing ashes of an incinerated world. The visionaries and seers do not simply map out symbolically and consecrate the established economy and politics of a community; they present another world. Neither the visions of Isaiah, Homer, Milton, and William Blake nor those of Simón Bolívar, Che Guevara, Mahatma Gandhi, and Nelson Mandela simply make the existing environment intelligible.

A myth does not extend its sway in multiple intellectual acts of synthesis. The *Ramayana* has for more than two thousand years been the dominant myth first in Hindu India, then in Hinayana Buddhist Myanmar, Thailand, Laos, and Cambodia, in Mahayana Buddhist Vietnam, and in Muslim Indonesia. It is maintained not, as in "the religions of the book," through reading and preaching but in dramatic performance. In traditional areas of these lands even today, the *Ramayana* is performed, from dusk to dawn, at prescribed auspicious dates. People do not go, like modern theatergoers, to watch the plot unfold and the motivations of the characters become clear; everyone knows the story from childhood. What draws them once again is also not a new interpretation, new staging, or new actors; the performers are indeed critically appraised, but in terms of the degree of their realization of timeless ideals. The people watch through the night in something of a trance state, in a state of possession, as Nietzsche said of ritual tragic theater in ancient Greece.

The shamans and healers do not simply effect the castration that destines the troubled one to the pursuit of the objects that the symbolic system of the community designates; they consecrate his alienation from the community, they make his voice heard to the community. How could they be the agents designated by the community to integrate someone stricken with idiosyncratic notions and physical unfitness into the reason and work of the community when the shaman is a heresiarch and a malingerer, when his or her visions improvise and his or her practices may be black magic? The visions of visionaries and seers call upon, call up powers that ordinary life in society does not awaken, that the symbolic system of the society does not elicit.

Žižek first depicted fantasies as a bricolage of symbols that are fitted into flaws and inconsistencies of the symbolic system of the culture in which we find ourselves. That is to envision symbols statically, as pieces of a system. It makes the essential activity at the core of an individual an activity of elaborating meaning. But our individuality is not constituted by a ceaseless spinning of an ever-wider spiderweb of intelligible relations.

In *The Plague of Fantasies*, Žižek says that fantasies provide desire with its coordinates and thus structure, channel, our desires.[1] More exactly, "fantasy space" is the template that converts the hungers and thirsts of life after what it needs into unlimited desires. The images in our fantasy space figure as symbols, symbols of the object *a*, of lack, of the irremediably absent object of desire. Invoking such an absent object, producing a symbol for it, would transform our wants and needs, always finite, always in principle satisfiable, into desire, desire for the infinite. This insatiable desire that does not know what it desires, that longs for the totality, for the infinite, is the Hegelian spirit in us. The spirit, thus conceived as a relay of the need that defines us as living organisms, is, Hegel said, negativity.

But a living organism is not an abyss; it is a dynamo. In being healthy, in being alive, our organisms generate energies in excess of what we need to satisfy our hungers and thirsts. In so much of what we do, awakening because our body is recharged overnight, dancing in the morning sunlight, going for a mountain hike on the weekend, we give without expectation of return. If fantasies are constituted by introjection, the objects we introject not only symbolize a desired completion and plenitude but also shatter systems of skills and psychic structures that had been stabilized in us and release excess energies.

Friedrich Nietzsche envisioned value terms in a new way, not as designations of properties of things nor as terms that function to compare and rank things but as confirmations and intensifications of surges of inner feeling. It is in exclamations—"How good I feel!" "How healthy I am!" "How real I feel!" "How beautiful I am!"—that these terms receive their sense. I say, "How healthy I am!" because I feel it, and in saying it I feel still more healthy. To feel healthy is not to have the essentially negative notion of no debility, no sickness that we shape from the doctor's (or our own, amateur doctor's) examination but to feel exultant energies to burn. The exclamation "How happy I am!" catches up a surge of exhilaration within, intensifies it, and makes it flare outward.

In impassioned experiences we uttered those words: I am a dancer! I am a mountaineer! I greet everyone with passionate kisses of parting! These words project radiant and captivating visions in us. Do not our visions—the visions of visionaries and seers, the visions of our youth, the visions generated by the word of honor we have planted in ourselves— function not to concoct the missing pieces that would make the symbolic system of our culture meaningful for ourselves but rather to confirm, consecrate, and intensify the surges of our strong feelings and impassioned states? Daniel Paul Schreber, in naming his anus solar glorifies his sense of its radiant seductiveness. Georges Bataille's obsessive image of a third eye, opening on top of his head to look directly into the sun, intensifies his boldest and most extravagant impulses. Such terms and visions do not get their sense from the context; they intensify our gratuitous forces and form incendiary points that blaze new paths and new contexts about them.

Žižek assumes that the forces mobilized by drive, which takes hold of an organ and compulsively makes it repeat the same failed gesture, aim at the excessive and monstrous paroxysm of pleasure in pain that is *jouissance*. He assumes that the forces mobilized by fantasy pant after the other who prohibits and therefore detains the forces of jouissance. Fantasy is illusionary, frail, and helpless, he thinks, because it has been detoured, and detoured without end, from drive. Should we not rather object that jouissance can never appear as something possible in the organism, not because it would be a death drive in a finite and temporal organism but because it is a by-product and not a goal?

The vision in us—I am a dancer! I am an adventurer! I am a revolutionary!—calls forth, intensifies, and consecrates the productive and sacrificial powers in us. The forces mobilized by a vision are not oriented toward pleasure nor the excessive and monstrous excesses of pleasure in pain; they aim at a work or an artwork, a revolution or a transfiguration. We know inwardly that we have kisses and caresses to squander on someone, have a tenderness and an excitement to give someone such as no lover has ever yet given anyone. We have the conviction felt in exhilaration of having the strength and the spirit to train and to inspire our body to dance as no one has ever before danced; we feel inwardly we have the heart and the nerves to endure all the risks, disasters, failures, and savageries of the revolution. The forces mobilized by a vision in an individual may well intensify the Promethean and reptilian strengths to endure the unintelligible and absurd destiny of a body born for or imprisoned in pain. Trapped, caged, straitjacketed, we know a will that shall not bend and the terrible force of our curses.

The strengths in life do not only seek out the radiant surfaces and open horizons; there is also a vehement urge to plunge into its dark depths. If we were to avoid the gaping chasms, the fractures and groundswells, the storm clouds, the sinkholes and fetid swamps, the moans of the suffering and the dying, we would, like Prince Siddhartha, sense that we were not in contact with reality, were skimming over the surfaces of things. We grieve over the corpse of the child, the fallen hero, the black-necked cranes whose remote breeding grounds are being logged or mined. To grieve is to hold our eyes open upon the loss and thus over the reality and worth of what was lost. It takes strength to grieve.

How can my voice be my own when it is formulated in the words and grammar of the common language? Heidegger's conception of "the talk" contains the notion that there are certain basic words in everyday talk (as well as in the philosophical tradition) and certain generalities that are repeated, relayed from one speaker to another. Flaubert's *Dictionary of Accepted Ideas*[2] set out to identify the statements and judgments taken as established by the bourgeoisie of his time. Recent critical theory that identifies the dominant discourse of a social class, employed to justify certain social practices and imposed by extralinguistic means, and cultural studies that contrast the rhetoric of the mass media with what is really the case—identified with the empirical findings of scientific economics, sociology, and psychology (although these too have "ideological" content)—work by identifying terms, symbols, and images that are the basic constants of the verbal or visual and musical language.

One who speaks on one's own, formulating insights about one's singular situation—Heidegger's authentic individual[3]—would invent neologisms or use vocabulary in new ways, put individual indexes on statements about the general lines of situations, create a personal style for literary and rhetorical genres, and even individualize grammar. The poets, and Heidegger's own texts, would be examples. Critical theory credits slang, street talk, and Black English for its ability to introduce concrete insights into the vocabulary and reasonings of the dominant discourse.

Yet when we do find our own voice, how striking that it is with the commonest words of language: "I am a man!" "I am a mother!" "I am young still!" Even those who speak with neologisms and stylize their grammar and rhetoric affirm that they have found their own voice in saying, "I am a thinker!" "I am a poet!"

The opposition between words and generalities incessantly repeated and an idiolect misconstrues the way language exists. Every language works with a limited phonetic system, but these phonemes give rise in speakers to unending variations of pitch, attack, duration, timbre, and volume. The syntactic system is not composed of a fixed set of forms; words generate plural forms, collect prefixes and suffixes, are inverted, and are agglutinated with other words; the paradigmatic form of an assertion, question, or exclamation produces variant forms. The semantic system assimilates foreign words and engenders new terms. A rhetorical style cannot be characterized by the use of constant terms and expressions but is identifiable as a style by the variations it generates. Even a discourse composed entirely of clichés puts them in a different order and succession and changes their force, intensity, and solidity by the passionate adhesion, skeptical tone, or ironic distance it takes in their regard. Individuals speak a common language, but the common language exists only in engendering individual voices.

Others recognize my voice as my own when, in its tone and force and in the times when I speak, they catch on to the force of my experiences and the intensity of my visions. But it is possible that my own voice remain secret. For every dancer, political leader, doctor, victim of a debilitating and terminal illness who tells his or her story in an interview, autobiography, or diary, there are millions who recount their story only to themselves. How many sons do not dare to pull out of their father in his last years the story he has kept for himself all his life!

Today's global media herald their achievement in giving a voice to the unimaginable numbers of humanity. Anyone can signal one's individuality by posting one's eccentric or violent message on the Internet. Celebrities are made with voices and gestures that are seductive to millions. There are celebrities who find their own voice in giving their voice to the unheard, in speaking for the distress and the dreams of the thirty-five million people in refugee camps, the millions whose voice is strangled by famine, is muffled behind prison walls, the millions of infants who will die of famine or AIDS before they can learn to speak. There they hear words unendingly repeated—"I am a mother!" "I am a man!" "I am young still!"—words of individuals incomparable and unforgettable.

23

The Representative Voice

Every established discourse of the sciences and technologies enlists individuals who in impassioned experience have recognized the sublimity of the astronomic, biological, or microscopic realm their science is exploring and mapping; the significance of agricultural research or pharmaceutical manufacture; the importance of institutions of justice and for care for the handicapped and infirm. In speaking and answering, they speak with the words of the established discourse; they stand in those words and find their own voice. They put their bodies and their lives in their responses. To be there, in the building, as electricians is to commit themselves to repair any blown circuit at any hour and wherever it is, even at risk to their bodies. There are risks to which an ophthalmologist, a ferryboat captain, and a public health nurse expose their clients, but they expose themselves to risks that may well be greater.

The importance of a group and its habitat, work, visions, and follies is also recognized in the talk of individuals. The ethnographer Kathleen Stewart listened, in what for her were impassioned experiences, to the talk of West Virginia unemployed people in abandoned coal-mining regions. She heard their individual voices and writes to convey them in their rhythms, accents, and silences.[1]

The talk of the people she recorded is "just talk"; it is not the canonical discourse of rational and technical knowledge, and it does not supply general paradigms of explanation. It recounts unforeseen events and accidents, effects disproportionate to their causes; it dramatizes singular events and invokes like events from an unforgettable or fabled past. What is "just talk" rummages in the space outside of completed thoughts and does not simply exemplify or fill out thoughts we have. Connections between things are always partial; there is always something more to say, always room for new questions, and associations form that are themselves unforeseen events. "Just talk," because it dramatizes unpredictable events and accidents and the eccentricity of behavior they and the stories told about them provoke, is amusement, and in the shared laughter and tears a community is formed and prized.

Stewart records not only the story but also the score of the story—reproducing as well as she can on her pages the rhythm, the periodicity, the pitch, and the accents of the voice. Are not the tropes of the stories told and the phantasms they quicken born from this musicality of the voice? The timbre, resonance, and rhythms of each voice make the plot of the stories told and retold each time different. In the way an individual tells the story of the drought and famine that ravaged the community, he makes the story of his own hunger and desperation his commitment to his community and to his word.

24

Eclipse

The story of the I is not the whole story. I act on my own when I am visited by what is important, and it reveals how it has to be urgently safeguarded, nourished, repaired, or brought into existence, and I recognize I am the one who is there and who has the resources. I speak with my own voice not continually but at moments when others come to assist me or to contest me. I find myself on my own in childbearing, combat, compulsions to divest myself of all that I have accumulated, traveling in strange lands, and in prison, refugee camps, the killing fields of malaria, tuberculosis, and AIDS.

The child to whom I have given my life lives now with her own life, irrevocably separated from me. The forest I have protected, the birds and fish I have nourished, the plants I have rescued from the weeds and the storms now flourish with their own inhuman energies. The paths, roads, and buildings I have built, the books I have written carry on their inert existence without me now and after my death and retain nothing of the pulse of my life.

The *Bhagavad-Gita* enjoins action without attachment to the results of action. It is the ethics of the doctor who must not falter although so many of his patients die; of the psychiatrist who continues to work with neurologically damaged, incurable patients; of the researcher who stays at her post the months and years that her work yields no results; of the adventurer who brings back nothing from his voyages but the scars of accidents and diseases.

I lose sight of myself, absorbed by the outbreak of a street fight, the coordinated operations of firefighters, the samba of street *carnaval*, the murmur of hospitality. In my intimate contact with external beings, their existence comes to invade me. In laughter before someone bungling and dysfunctional, my own body becomes indulgent of and indulges in the dissolution of its working mobilizations; in tears the loss of a friend, the death of an animal wild and free, or the destruction of an ancient building or an archive is my own loss. In orgasm the lover's dissolute laughter and spasms of torment and pleasure invade me and overwhelm my sense of myself; in orgy my self-control and self-respect are triumphantly dissolved. In the laughter and tears of conversation, in feasting, in carnivals, and in collective anger over injustice, I dissolve in waves of life no more separate than the waves of the sea. I give up the posture that mobilizes my body to become a prolongation of the lunge or saunter of the horse I ride, or to float among the fish in the coral seas. In the meadow and the forest I am invaded by the stirring of plants emerging from the ground and unfolding in the sun. In the night the darkness invades me, extinguishing my positions taken before things, dissolving me in the beginningless, endless oncoming of existence, the sea of tranquillity.

25

To Know and to Acknowledge

The word of honor we put on ourselves is not a word addressed to anyone. It is not a response to a question or a demand others put to us. Yet the "I" of "I am a man," "For my part, I think . . ." makes itself understood. With greetings, appeals, blessings, insults, and curses, in trust and courage, contact is made with you.

There are times when we have to speak up, with our own voice. There are dangers we have to forestall. There are people we have to avoid lest they poison our lives with their authority or their cynicism. There are people we have to drive off or strike down. The doctor heading for the refugee camp has to confront government and bandit roadblocks that demand his supplies.

The power to fix a word in ourselves, to fix ourselves with a word, makes us responsible, able to answer for what we say and do. It makes us able to make promises, to undertake commitments to others. The you I address is a force that addresses the me who says "Let me tell you . . . ," questions the me who says "I will go," makes demands on the dancer I say I am, contests the youth I say I still am, puts me and my situation in the midst of the common world in question. The response that I make to you I address to you for your judgment.

We do not always have to speak to others when we are among them; we do not have to explain to others our laughter and our tears, our blessings and our curses. We do not have to justify our pleasure in being healthy, with energy to burn, our pleasure coming upon, in the crotch of a cactus, a hummingbird nest woven out of spiderwebs and containing two minuscule eggs. We do not owe them an explanation of our grief over a fawn found dead on a woodland path or our grief over the betrayed dreams of our youth. We do not owe others a justification of all that we have done and said; we do not owe them a justification of our word of honor, our fantasy space, the story of our life. We owe no one a justification for our being there, for being alive, for craving to love. Not even God.

It is to those we have wronged that we must speak. We must recognize their shame, anger, and suffering and acknowledge the injustice, injury, and harm we have done to them. Only then do we make contact with who they are.

Acknowledgment is forestalled by interpreting what we did and said and explaining our intentions. It is circumvented by our effort to know our conscious and our unconscious motives.

The distress, anguish, mortification of another is exposed to us in the spasms, the wounds, the scars, and the wrinkles of his or her skin. Opening our eyes upon the wounds and scars, our eyes make contact with his or her pain, which afflicts us immediately, invading our look, making us wince with the acuteness of that pain. The suffering of the one who faces me, visible in the bloodless white of her anguished face, may well be not the suffering of her own hunger and thirst but a suffering for children or animals of other species in her care, farms and forests he cares for, archives and memories of her people she cherishes.

We have to acknowledge the wrong we have done to another by our actions or omissions but also the wrong we ourselves did not initiate or foresee, the wrongs done by the government we elect and obey and which never acknowledges the harm done by domestic policies and foreign wars conducted in our name, the wrongs done to children and neighbors and people in far-off lands whose ignorance and destitution are maintained by our prosperity. We have to know. Here to speak truthfully is imperative. We have to acknowledge the wrong, in words spoken without mental reservations, but also in gestures or even in reticence, the silence that silences our impulse to explain.

Part 9

Dishonor

26

To Thine Own Self Untrue

Scientific work involves the possibility of a researcher devoting the exceptional powers of his or her mind and years, decades, of work on a mistaken hypothesis and faulty evidence. The most gifted statesmen devote their energies to secondary or diversionary issues. Not the common judgment nor the judgment of those taken as experts but our deepening intimacy with the topic or field of action, our heightened perceptual and conceptual sensitivity, our logical acumen, breadth and depth of comprehension, and capacity to distinguish the important from the trivial will determine whether we are or are not mistaken.

We can be mistaken about our resources, insights, skills, and energies. All the testing done in universities and conservatories does not establish that we will one day be a thinker, a dancer. We can stay on as dancers, teachers, doctors, mothers, despite our incompetence, refusing to recognize or recognizing that incompetence.[1]

Before the fear of not having the resources, insights, skills, and energies to realize the work to which we have pledged ourself, we provide ourself with an alibi from the start. We get married, having decided to devote all our life and erotic resources on just this one person, but we start right away working to get a promotion and buying a house and a boat, or having a baby, less the fruit of our love than a compensation for the possible trailing off of love. We go into pure science with the secret idea that we will contribute something of our own. We sense that somewhere about midlife, it will become clear if we have the talent and the devotion or if we are just another academic hack—with another twenty years until retirement, knowing that, the students knowing that. From the start, we get something else going: acquire a demanding household, devote ourself to teaching and administrative policies.

We can shift our sense of the important to "positional goods"[2]—goods such that it is materially or even logically impossible for more than a few to have them. Great sums of money can become the way to keep score; public acclaim and honors replace contact with what is important and sublime. The self-taught outsider artist, driven by his ecstasies or his rage to create a metaphysical habitat for himself, is recognized by critics, collectors, galleries, and museums and begins to paint to acquire celebrity and wealth. The pursuit of positional goods excludes other impassioned experiences. Avarice excludes anger, grief, or falling in love, which interrupt and engulf the attention to the predictable future. It excludes shame, regret, and mourning that are concerned with our own past.[3]

We can commit ourselves to the unknowability or the inexistence of the important. Cynicism prides itself on its superior lucidity. Recognizing self-interest to be intrinsic to human nature, the human species to be essentially predatory, we resign ourselves to the sound and fury of marketplace and battlefield. Considering the human species from the evolutionary or cosmic point of view, we feel no anger or grief before floods, earthquakes, and plagues. We can live an opportunistic and self-indulgent life made of acquiescences, compromises, and resignations.

Professional Dishonor

Individuals passionately commit their resources, insights, energies, skills, and honor to what is identified as important in the rational discourse of a scientific discipline or technological practice or in the common language of their, or another, community. The established discourse discredits as incompetent and unfit those who do not represent well and with honor the established truth. The professional honor of a scientific researcher, a lawyer, a doctor, or an engineer may be specified in a code of professional conduct. Those whose practice is not ordered by the established discourse bring dishonor to the profession.

The established discourse and the code of professional conduct can limit and even dislodge our experience of what is important and urgent. Speaking the established discourse of a researcher seeking funding, a social worker, or a uniformed patrol officer can displace the story we tell ourselves about our visions, energies, and competence. "This is what science says"—and the doctor relinquishes his or her responsibility and very identity as a healer. We can find that the established discourse takes over our voice and orders our actions, such that a social worker, a computer programmer, or a professor feels he or she begins to live only after hours or after retirement.

We may discover that the established discourse about what is important is incomplete or faulty or that the established discourse of the institution or community covers over practices that deny or betray that to which we have committed ourselves. Political leaders learn a rhetoric of justification out of loyalty to the party.[1] A researcher working in a pharmaceutical laboratory sees that the company is lobbying the government to suppress generic variants of its products in impoverished countries devastated by disease. Conflict between betraying our sense of honor as an artist, a healer, or an educator and dishonoring the institution is an eventuality inherent in every institution, as conflict between betraying our sense of honor as a parent or a caretaker of part of the land and work and dishonoring the community is a possibility in every community.

The established discourse of a collective can accord an attributed honor to someone who occupies a position in the collective without fulfilling or being able to fulfill his or her tasks. He or she can use the attributed honor to attain venal or cynical ends. The honor attributed to the position and established in discourse makes corruption possible.

The Established Dishonor

The discourse of a collective establishes what that collective takes to be true and what false. Every established discourse—established by watchwords, passwords, and prompts or established by the decrees of experts—determines what observations and what arguments could be valid and those that are invalid. The discourse of scientific medicine has determined in advance that talk of the plague being the work of an offended deity cannot be true. For the law and the police, the inner-city gang is possessed by false values. The discourse of "society" determines what vocabulary and tropes are appropriate and what inappropriate; the watchwords of the pack determine what is cool.

The collective may recognize a plurality of discourses as valid. The medical team gives the nurse time off to honor commitments to a lover or to ailing parents back home. Free speech may be established by an institution and a community because what individuals may say out of their insights might one day be recognized to contribute to the established discourse, or because deviant talk is deemed harmless or can be neutralized by the ridicule that affirms the reason of the institution or the common sense of the community.

The watchwords and passwords of a collective also decree when an individual is excluded from the collective work, defense, research, or adventures and follies. The scientific community pronounces the verdict "charlatan." For "society," she is henceforth a bore; for the work team, he is a complainer; for the police, this youth is a troublemaker, this adult a delinquent.

Individuals within the work or research team, "society," or gang may meet the outsider and hear his story and indeed engage with him for what he finds important: the workers cover for the woman who steals to pay for her abortion; the prison guard allows the resistance fighter to escape. The collective may decree that she is a good poet but an incompetent notary, that he is a reliable neighbor when needed, though a libertine.

The grammar of English determines what combinations of English words do not make sense; the symbol system and axiomatics of geometry determine what combinations cannot be mathematically functional; the vocabulary, grammar, and methodology of mechanics determine what explanations can only be nonsense. The fundamental community decisions as to what could count as observations, what standards of accuracy in determining observations are possible, and what could count as an argument determine what statements and what actions do not make sense at all.[1]

The established discourse of the European Middle Ages excluded those identified as heretics; today's established discourse excludes those identified as religious fanatics or delusional neurotics. One cannot reason with them; whatever they say is rejected with derision. Those outside the community with whom its established discourse could not communicate were identified during the Enlightenment as idolaters, savages, and cannibals; they do not answer for what they say and do to our community but communicate with each other in ways irrational to us or communicate with beasts and demons. Today they are identified as terrorists, communicating not with us but with their inner demons.

The words of the excluded, passionately committed to their experiences, do get heard outside the walls of exclusion and even after they have been liquidated. To definitively silence them, they have to be made to repudiate their words and deeds. Criminals who exhibit remorse at their trials and inform on their accomplices are promised leniency. The methods of counseling and psychoanalysis—in most cases imposed under court action or threat of court action—aim to induce the fanatic to concede the truth of the psychiatric-juridical discourse that has identified him or her as psychotic.

What is demanded of the fanatic, psychotic, and terrorist is that he or she acknowledge that he or she does not have a mind capable of contributing to or verifying the truth of the collective. What is expected is that he or she admits to being incapable of truth, confesses that her or his mind is corrupt, her or his body driven by vile compulsions. The demonstration is made with confinement, electric shocks, and drugs in insane asylums; with sleep deprivation, beatings, electrical shocks, and forced sexual acts that traumatize the body in prisons; and with solitary confinement in maximum-security prisons that derange any mind.

Part 10

Pariahs

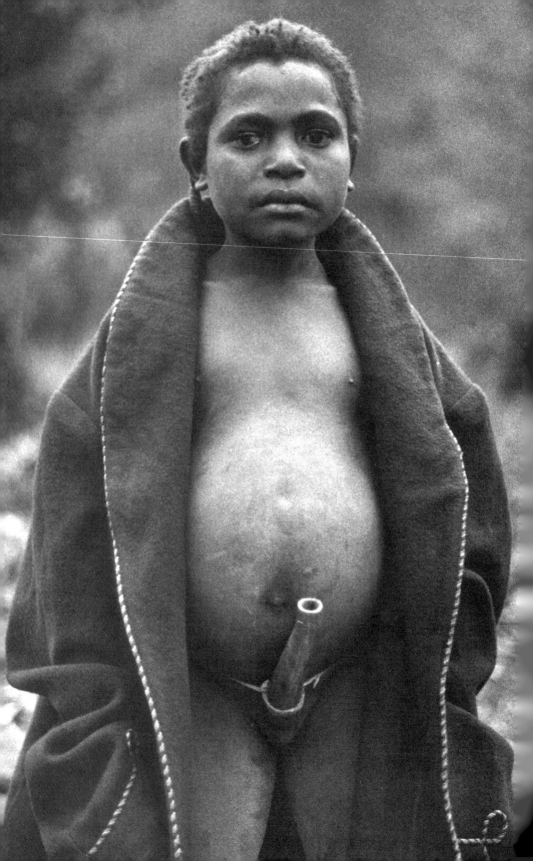

Outcast Honor

Incarcerated in an insane asylum, Daniel Paul Schreber wrote his *Memoirs of My Nervous Illness*[1] to exclude in advance all the ways the court that was put in charge of his affairs and the psychiatrists who were put in charge of his mental state understood him. By entitling his account memoirs "of my nervous illness," he excluded in advance all the ways we who do not share his nervous hyperexcitability could understand his thoughts, which he elaborated into a cosmic religion. His *Grundsprache* (fundamental language) was instead a language picked up from birds and addressed to birds.

In prison, men and women who have been marked with dishonor by the community respond with contempt for the values incarnated in the judges and wardens they know, clamp a mask of "cool" or self-assurance on their faces, and threaten with violence any violation of the integrity of their word and experience from fellow prisoners. Their body, its drives and its forces, harbors their honor.[2]

What resists the confession the torturer demands is not the character or will of the captive; militants carry vials of arsenic because they know that torturers can crush all character and break any will. What resists, as the torturer reduces the captive's body to sexual degradation and spilled blood and gore, shit, is the captive's word of honor given to his comrades in a struggle where many will be doomed, and to those for whom he fought and who will suffer when the cause is lost and whose anger will be reborn. In the darkness the rats that penetrate the walls are his comrades. His body commits its pain and decomposition to the cement of the dungeon walls in which his screams and sobs are muffled, to the rock strata of the silent planet into which they sink. Even as he confesses his dishonor, his presence whispers his word of honor to the rats and rocks and stars.

The tragic theater of ancient Greece had developed from participationist trance rituals. After their victory in the Trojan War, Athenians watched and participated in Euripides' *Trojan Women*, a play that presented nothing but the outcries and lamentations of their defeated enemies.

In the first World War, 90 percent of the killed and wounded were combatants; in the Korean War, only 40 percent were combatants; in the wars of the last two decades, 90 percent of the killed and wounded have been noncombatants.[3] The terrorist campaign of the strong was launched in the nuclear incineration of 450,000 in Hiroshima and Nagasaki. Alain Renais's film *Hiroshima Mon Amour* invited the victors to watch, to participate in, the screams of their victims.

Renais's film also invites his French audience to participate in the open wounds of a Frenchwoman who loved a German soldier. Jean Genet's *Funeral Rites* commemorates his love also for a German officer of the occupation, his treasonous love. Genet's funeral rites are devised to steal away the body of his executed lover from collective ignominy in liberated France and collective honor in his homeland and entomb him in Genet's body.

To make contact with another is to break through that person's integrity, nature, independence, autonomy—to violate him or her. Contact takes place when we risk ourselves, each of us putting ourself and the other in the region of death and nothingness. Those who go make contact with fanatics, psychotics, and terrorists find that something outside the imperative for law—strange powers, demonic, cosmic—that we do not understand rules in them. Antipsychiatrists who go live with psychotics, the doctors without borders and reporters without borders, pro bono lawyers defending the perpetrators of abject crimes find that they violate those they seek to help and expose themselves to being violated, outraged, wounded by them.

Doctors and nurses, truck drivers, reporters working among the enemy populations terrorized and bombed, with the enemy soldiers incarcerated and tortured, with the millions in refugee camps, with the millions ravaged by famine and plague, performing surgeries in dusty tents, distributing sacks of food, nursing children dying of AIDS are themselves lacerated by the wounds of the enemy, ravaged by the starvation of the victims of famine. They find that their work separates them from their own nation and people. Their word of honor is a betrayal of the cause of the war, of the prosperity of their nation.

Each of us has this to do: to die. As we witness the deaths of others, we note how they died: with bravery and silent resolve, with patience and endurance, spending what strengths they had to settle unresolved affairs, to attend to the needs of the works and loved ones who will survive them; or cowardly, clinging and calling upon the pity of others, whimpering and despairing. How we die is a word we address to others. We also know that the strengths or weaknesses with which we die are those with which we live. It can happen that out of our present despair we destroy what we have built, and that gave us and others hope, out of our present bitterness we destroy the bonds of affection and generosity that had given us family and friends. It can happen that we can do nothing in living but can do much in dying.

Notes

Chapter 1

1. Friedrich Nietzsche, *Thus Spoke Zarathustra,* trans. Walter Kaufmann in *The Portable Nietzsche* (New York: Viking, 1968), I, "On Free Death," 183.

Chapter 2

1. Emmanuel Levinas calls this density of supporting and sustaining reality "the elemental." *Totality and Infinity,* trans. Alphonso Lingis (Pittsburgh: Duquesne University Press, 1969), 130–42.

2. Thus one could come to think of life as the force of lack and need that develop in the material composition of an organism and that animate its perception and activate its movements. Georg Friedrich Hegel conceived of all consciousness as the force of negativity. Immanuel Kant defined the happiness that life pursues as the complete and permanent satisfaction of all needs and wants. The sense of oneself that arises in a living organism arises in need and aims at satisfaction.

3. Martin Heidegger, *Being and Time,* trans. John Macquarrie and Edward Robinson (New York: Harper and Row, 1962), 95–102.

4. Philip Fisher, *The Vehement Passions* (Princeton, N.J.: Princeton University Press, 2002), 6–7.

5. Albert O. Hirschman, *The Passions and the Interests* (Princeton, N.J.: Princeton University Press, 1981), 42–66.

Chapter 3

1. Levinas, *Totality and Infinity,* 152–54.

2. Ibid., 158–62.

3. Heidegger, *Being and Time,* 114–22. Alphonso Lingis, "The World as a Whole," in *Sensations: Intelligibility in Sensibility* (Atlantic Highlands, N.J.: Humanities Press, 1996), 13–29.

4. *Vorhanden:* Heidegger, *Being and Time,* 102–4.

5. A. R. Luria, *The Nature of Human Conflicts* (New York: Liveright, 1976).

6. Giles Deleuze and Félix Guattari, *A Thousand Plateaus*, trans. Brian Massumi (Minneapolis: University of Minnesota Press, 1987), 311–50.

7. Luria, *Nature of Human Conflicts*.

8. "The true ideal would be the restoration of a 'natural' rhythm and movement, the 'kinetic melody' (in Luria's term) natural and normal to each particular patient: something which would not be a mere scheme or diagram or algorithm of behaviour, but a restoration of genuine spaciousness and freedom. We have seen, again and again, that patients' own kinetic melodies *can* be given back to them, albeit briefly, by the use of an appropriate flow of *music*. . . .Other 'natural' motions of Nature and Art are equally potent if experienced visually or tactually. Thus, I have known patients almost totally immobilised by Parkinsonism, dystonias, contortions, etc., capable of riding a horse with ease—with ease and grace and intuitive control, forming with the horse a mutually influencing and natural unity; indeed, the mere *sight* of riding, running, walking, swimming, of any natural movement whatever—as a purely visual experience on a television screen— can call forth by sympathy, or suggestion, an equal naturalness of movement in Parkinsonian patients. The art of 'handling' Parkinsonian patients, learned by sensitive nurses and friends—assisting them by the merest intimation or touch, or by a wordless, touchless moving-together, in an intuitive kinetic sympathy of attunement—this is a genuine art, which can be exercised by a man or a horse or a dog, but which can *never* be simulated by any mechanical feedback; for it is only an ever-changing, melodic, and living play of forces which can recall *living* beings into their own living being. Such a subtle, ever-changing play of forces may also be achieved through the use of certain 'natural' devices, which *intermediate,* so to speak, between afflicted patients and the forces of Nature. Thus while severely affected Parkinsonians are particularly dangerous at the controls of motorcars and motorboats (which tend to amplify all their pathological tendencies), they may be able to handle a sailing boat with ease and skill, with an intuitive accuracy and 'feel.' Here, in effect, man-boat-wind-wave come together in a natural, dynamic union or unison; the man feels at one, at home, with the forces of Nature; his own natural melody is evoked by, attuned to, the harmony of Nature; he ceases to be a *patient*—passive and pulsive—and is transformed to an *agent*—active and free." (Oliver Sacks, *Awakenings* [London: Picador, 1991], 348–49)

9. Aristotle, *Rhetoric*, 2.8.1386a15–20.

10. Fisher, *Vehement Passions*, 39.

11. Ibid., 88.

12. Friedrich Nietzsche, *The Gay Science*, trans. Walter Kaufmann (New York: Vintage, 1974), ¶333.

13. They also, Deleuze and Guattari observe, make our body a territory; they mark frontiers others do not cross. Their gaze stands apart from the tattooed body, viewing it from a distance. *Thousand Plateaus*, 320.

Chapter 4

1. Martin Heidegger, *On the Way to Language,* trans. Peter D. Hertz (New York: Harper and Row, 1971), 155 and passim.

Chapter 5

1. Telling stories are means of understanding; the most common way to understand an entity or an event is to recount a story about it. Stories are explanations; they trace out the situation of a thing or event in a network of prior relevant circumstances and events. Formal education may proceed largely by descriptions, listings, classifications, arguments, models, and charts. But most of our parallel or subsequent learning about our practical and social environment consists in hearing stories and revising and expanding the stock of stories we have acquired. Cf. Roger C. Shank and Tamara R. Berman, "The Pervasive Role of Stories in Knowledge and Action," in *The Narrative Impact,* ed. Melanie C. Green, Jeffrey J. Strange, and Timothy C. Brock (Mahwah, N.J.: Lawrence Erlbaum, 2002), 287.

2. Paul Feyerabend, *Against Method* (London: Verso, 1984), 36–46.

Chapter 6

1. Deleuze and Guattari, *Thousand Plateaus,* 387–94.

Chapter 7

1. Bernard Williams, *Ethics and the Limits of Philosophy* (Cambridge, Mass.: Harvard University Press, 1985), 182.

2. Friedrich Nietzsche, *Beyond Good and Evil,* trans. Walter Kaufmann (New York: Vintage, 1966), ¶257.

3. Heidegger, *Being and Time,* 114–15.

4. The maximum power of hummingbirds is 133 watts per kilogram of muscle; it is 15 watts per kilogram of muscle for humans.

5. David Hume, *A Treatise of Human Nature* (Garden City, N.Y.: Doubleday, 1961), 423.

6. Immanuel Kant, *Fundamental Principles of the Metaphysic of Morals,* trans. Thomas K. Abbott (Indianapolis: Bobbs-Merrill, 1949), 11–16.

7. Immanuel Kant, *Critique of Judgment,* trans. Werner S. Pluhar (Indianapolis: Hackett, 1987), 114–17.

8. Kant, *Fundamental Principles of the Metaphysic of Morals,* 31–35.

Chapter 8

1. Friedrich Nietzsche, *On the Genealogy of Morals,* trans. Walter Kaufmann and R. J. Hollingdale (New York: Vintage, 1969), II, 2.

2. Leslie Farber, *Lying, Despair, Jealousy, Envy, Sex, Suicide, Drugs and the Good Life* (New York: Basic Books, 1976), 7.

3. Belinda Thompson, ed., *Gauguin by Himself* (Boston: Little, Brown and Company, 1993), 270.

4. Nietzsche, *Beyond Good and Evil,* ¶ 40.

5. David Abram, personal communication.

6. Jon Elster, *Sour Grapes: Studies in the Subversion of Rationality* (Cambridge: Cambridge University Press, 1987), 153.

Chapter 9

1. As we walk, we cannot look at our gait, even in a mirror, for the observing eye itself which has redirected itself interferes with the gaze that accompanied our walk down the street and alters our gait. Yet while walking, we have a sense of how we look: when a psychologist projects a videotape of people in silhouette walking across the landscape, we find we can pick out ourself from among them by the gait.

2. Melanie Klein, *The Selected Melanie Klein,* ed. Juliet Mitchell (New York: Free Press, 1987), 189–91.

3. "Even at the moment of the most intense bodily contact with each other, lovers are not alone, they need a minimum of phantasmic narrative as a symbolic support—that is, they can never simply 'let themselves go' and immerse themselves in 'that' . . ." Slavoj Žižek, *The Plague of Fantasies* (London: Verso, 1999), 65.

4. Nietzsche, *Thus Spoke Zarathustra,* III, 30, 2.

Chapter 10

1. "Recent experimental data support the claim that linguistic-semantic knowledge coded in the neural lexicon is real-world knowledge. . . . The PET data of Martin et al. [A. Martin, A. C. L. Wiggs, and L. G. Ungerleider, 'Discrete Cortical Regions Associated with Knowledge of Color and Knowledge of Action,' *Science* 270 (1995): 102–5] show that the primary motor cortex, implicated in manual motor control, is activated when we think of the name of a hand tool. Primary visual cortical areas associated with the perception of shape or color are activated when we think of the name of an animal. The activation of the primary visual cortex shows that thinking about a word enlists the neural structures that play a part in forming one aspect of the concept coded in the word, the shape or shapes and colors of the object of living being coded by the world. . . . The PET data of Martin and his colleagues show that tool names also activated a left

premotor area that was also activated by imagined hand movements as well as an area in the left middle temporal gyrus also activated by action words." (Philip Lieberman, *Human Language and Our Reptilian Brain* [Cambridge, Mass.: Harvard University Press, 2000], 62–63)

Chapter 11

1. The philosophy of mind, whether working with Locke's, Kant's, or Husserl's analysis, has depicted ego-identity as the passive or active retention of past events in memory.

2. Sartre's "fundamental project" or Heidegger's "resoluteness." Jean-Paul Sartre, *Being and Nothingness,* trans. Hazel E. Barnes (New York: Washington Square Press, 1966) 723–34; Martin Heidegger, *Being and Time,* 297–301.

3. "The so-called talking cure is a joint effort by patient and therapist to articulate the story of the patient in such a way that what has been unspeakable so far can at last be said; what had to be a secret can now be revealed; what had to be forgotten can be remembered; what had to be endured and survived can be mourned and grieved; what had been passed over in silence and solitude can be carefully examined, attended to and shared in the company of a loving, empathic other. Therapy, like storytelling, is an oral (and aural) art. R.D. Laing used to coach his patients to tell their stories over and over, until they themselves could describe and depict the most painful and horrendous events without dissolving into tears. He thought that by the time you can deliver your history so that others will weep, not you yourself, you would feel healed and ready to get on with your life without a chip on your shoulders." (Andrew Feldmar, "The Truth About Stories: A Native Narrative," *In a Nutshell* [Winter 2004], 7)

4. Nietzsche, *Gay Science,* ¶360.

5. "For one thing is needful: that a human being should *attain* satisfaction with himself, whether it be by means of this or that poetry and art. . . . Whoever is dissatisfied with himself is continually ready for revenge, and we others will be his victims, if only by having to endure his ugly sight. For the sight of what is ugly makes one bad and gloomy." Ibid., ¶290.

6. Ibid., ¶299.

7. Ibid.

8. Nietzsche, *Thus Spoke Zarathustra,* IV, 3.

9. "When the oppressed, downtrodden, outraged exhort one another with the vengeful cunning of impotence: 'let us be different from the evil, namely good! And he is good who does not outrage, who harms nobody, who does not attack, who does not requite, who leaves revenge to God, who keeps himself hidden as we do, who avoids evil and desires little from life, like us, the patient, humble, and just'—this listened to calmly and without previous bias, really amounts to no more than: 'we weak ones are, after all, weak; it would be good if we did nothing *for which we are not strong enough*' . . ." Nietzsche, *Genealogy of Morals,* I:13.

Chapter 13

1. Nietzsche, *Genealogy of Morals.*
2. Susan Sontag, *Illness as Metaphor* (New York: Anchor, 1989).
3. Paul West, *A Stroke of Genius* (New York: Viking, 1995), 2.
4. Ibid., 71–73.
5. Paul West, *Out of My Depths* (New York: Doubleday, 1983), 83.
6. Paul West, *The Place in Flowers Where Pollen Rests* (New York: Collier, 1989), 97.
7. West, *Out of My Depths,* 16.
8. Nietzsche, *Gay Science,* ¶ 299.
9. Nietzsche, *Thus Spoke Zarathustra,* III, "The Convalescent," 2.
10. West, *Stroke of Genius,* 105.
11. Ibid., 92.

Chapter 14

1. Douglas W. Mock, *Behavior and Evolution of Birds: Readings from "Scientific American"* (New York: W. H. Freeman, 1991), 7–19.
2. Robert B. Payne, *Sexual Selection, Lek and Arena Behavior, and Sexual Size Dimorphism in Birds* (Washington, D.C.: American Ornithologists' Union, 1984), 1–2.
3. Jaak Panksepp, "Beyond a Joke: From Animal Laughter to Human Joy?" *Science,* April 1, 2005, 62–63.
4. "The passions track and locate a domain of the highest cultural worth, a domain shared with animals, who also, for example, not only fear and panic, or attack with rage, but mourn their losses. It is by means of the vehement states that what we might call the moral life of animals, their relation to power, to their own will, to their losses and pleasures, occurs in ways humans have always felt confident that they can interpret." Fisher, *Vehement Passions,* 24–25.

Chapter 16

1. Gustave Flaubert, *Madame Bovary,* trans. Eleanor Marx-Aveling (New York: Pocket Books, 1948), 308.
2. Sacks, *Awakenings,* 214–15 n. 101.
3. "Who is that?" we ask. "Who are you?" In recognizing someone we say, "You're Diane; we met last year in Toulouse." "You must be Paul, the repairman I spoke with on the phone?" The identity we recognize is a narrative identity; it is someone of whom we recount a succession of feelings, thoughts, and actions. The identity we recognize is the single linear or multistranded plot of a story. Already someone to whom a name is given is someone of whom a brief story is begun: "That's Judy over there, with the cowboy hat." "I am Sheila; I have just arrived from Aotearoa."

The identity we thus recognize in someone is a practical identity, an identity we use in recognizing someone at different times, in different situations, an identity we recognize in order to know how to approach and how to interact with him or her.

4. Immanuel Kant said what commands our respect for other people is the evidence that they exist on their own. They do so, he said, as rational agents. A rational agent is not just driven this way and that by external lures and internal unconscious drives and instincts. He is also not deluded by fantasies. What we respect in others is their rational faculty, the power in them to lead their own lives according to what they understand.

But sound reasons are everywhere the same. A rational person would judge any situation just as any other rational person would. According to Kant's conception, what we really respect is the universal rational faculty, and not persons in their individuality. There would be no such thing as respect for individuals as such.

Chapter 17

1. We speak of "trusting" the mechanical condition of the car, "trusting" the solidity of the scaffolding we set out to climb. More properly we would say that we expect or believe that the car will make the trip to the West Coast, that the iron-pipe scaffolding is solid. Our expectation is attached to the laws of nature. When we speak of "trusting" our car, it is because we view it as an old friend.

2. Homer's *Iliad* was for Aristotle as for his contemporaries the fullest account of human behaviors and capabilities. Aristotle did maintain courage as a military virtue, denying that those who confront death in shipwrecks, natural disasters, or fatal diseases could properly be called courageous, for they do not exhibit prowess, do not act and only wait passively, and do not choose since they do not have the alternative of flight. Courage for Aristotle is the force that drives men to slaughter other men at the risk of their own lives. Even today we rarely call anyone a coward except the one who flees the battlefield—a vice though without viciousness. For Aristotle the courage of the warrior—combining prowess, skill, energy, choice, and action—should characterize the work of citizens in the city-state, who each are ready to enlist in the citizen army when the occasion arises. Today soldiers who slaughter other men at the risk of their own lives are called courageous, though the war be declared on false evidence and for reasons of military or economic expansion and the soldiers be deluded or pressured to prove they are men. (There are no monuments to the dead of natural disasters, tsunamis, and plagues.)

Chapter 18

1. Deleuze and Guattari, *Thousand Plateaus*, 79–85.
2. Heidegger, *Being and Time*, 149–68.

3. Oscar Lewis, *The Children of Sanchez* (Harmondsworth, Eng.: Penguin, 1979).

4. Michel Foucault, *The History of Sexuality,* vol. 1, *An Introduction* (New York: Vintage, 1990), 94–102.

5. Feyerabend, *Against Method,* 141–43.

6. "For if, when I make some statement, it is true that nothing whatever could in fact be produced as a cogent ground for retracting it, this can only be because I am in, have got myself into, the very best possible position for making that statement—I have, and am entitled to have, *complete* confidence in it when I make it. But whether this is so or not is not a matter of what *kind of sentence* I use in making my statement, but of what *the circumstances are* in which I make it. If I carefully scrutinize some patch of colour in my visual field, take careful note of it, know English well, and pay scrupulous attention to just what I'm saying, I may say, 'It seems to me now as if I were seeing something pink'; and nothing whatever could be produced as showing that I had made a mistake. But equally, if I watch for some time an animal a few feet in front of me, in a good light, if I prod it perhaps, sniff, and take note of the noises it makes, I may say, 'That's a pig'; and this too will be 'incorrigible,' nothing could be produced that would show that I had made a mistake. Once one drops the idea that there is a special *kind of sentence* which is *as such* incorrigible, one might as well admit (what is plainly true anyway) that *many* kinds of sentences may be uttered in making statements which are *in fact* incorrigible—in the sense that, when they are made, the circumstances are such that they are quite certainly, definitely, and un-retractably *true.*" (J. L. Austin, *Sense and Sensibilia* [New York: Oxford University Press, 1964], 114–15)

Chapter 19

1. Deleuze and Guattari, *Thousand Plateaus,* 107–8.

Chapter 20

1. Richard Moran, *Authority and Estrangement* (Princeton, N.J.: Princeton University Press, 2001), 83–94.

2. Nietzsche, *Gay Science,* ¶354.

3. Deleuze and Guattari, *Thousand Plateaus,* 167–73.

Chapter 21

1. Claude Lévi-Strauss, *Structural Anthropology,* trans. Claire Jacobson and Brooke Grundfest Schoepf (New York: Basic Books, 1963), 186–205.

2. Kant, *Fundamental Principles of the Metaphysic of Morals,* 50–57.

3. "Avoid as much as possible any violation of the fantasy space of the other, i.e., respect as much as possible the other's 'particular absolute,' the way he orga-

nizes his universe of meaning in a way absolutely particular to him. Such an ethic is neither imaginary (the point is not to love our neighbor as ourselves, insofar as he resembles ourselves, i.e., insofar as we see in him an image of ourselves) nor symbolic (the point is also not to respect the other on account of the dignity bestowed on him by his symbolic identification, by the fact that he belongs to the same symbolic community as ourselves, even if we conceive this community in the widest possible sense and maintain respect for him 'as a human being'). What confers on the other the dignity of a 'person' is not any universal-symbolic feature but precisely what is 'absolutely particular' about him, his fantasy, that part of him that we can be sure we can never share. To use Kant's terms: we do not respect the other on account of the universal moral law inhabiting each of us, but on account of his utmost 'pathological' kernel, on account of the absolutely particular way each of us 'dreams his world,' organizes his enjoyment. . . .

"Fantasy as a 'make-believe' masking a flaw, an inconsistency in the symbolic order, is always particular—its particularity is absolute; it resists 'mediation,' it cannot be made part of a larger, universal, symbolic medium. For this reason, we can acquire a sense of the dignity of another's fantasy only by assuming a kind of distance toward our own, by experiencing the ultimate contingency of fantasy as such, by apprehending it as the way everyone, in a manner proper to each, conceals the impasse of his desire. The dignity of a fantasy consists in its very 'illusionary,' fragile, helpless character." (Slavoj Žižek, *Looking Awry: An Introduction to Jacques Lacan through Popular Culture* [Cambridge, Mass.: MIT Press, 1992], 156–57)

4. Ibid.

5. Immanuel Kant, *Critique of Practical Reason*, trans. Lewis White Beck (Indianapolis: Bobbs-Merrill, 1956), 24–25.

6. Žižek, *Looking Awry*, 157.

7. Ibid.

8. Ibid.

9. Ibid.

10. Slavoj Žižek, *The Plague of Fantasies* (London: Verso, 1997), 81.

11. Ibid., 9.

12. Ibid., 49.

13. Ibid., 65.

14. Ibid., 39.

15. Ibid.

16. Ibid., 21.

17. Slavoj Žižek, *The Ticklish Subject* (London: Verso, 1999), 391–92.

Chapter 22

1. Žižek, *Plague of Fantasies*, 7.

2. Gustave Flaubert, *Dictionary of Accepted Ideas*, trans. Jacques Barzun (New York: New Directions, 1968).

3. The phenomenological philosophy of Edmund Husserl had as its mission

to return to, to recover the original insights at the basis of rational culture—and all insights exist in the first person singular. To speak with my own voice is to formulate insights into my own situation. In perception our eyes catch on to a flash of color, a density in the flow of patterns, focus in on it and approach it, shift about it, until its sides stabilize and hold together. Then we see a real thing unmistakably present and we can say that it is and what it is. Yet we see it from only one side, and its reality and identity are suspended on a continued series of completions and confirmations. Heidegger replaced the intuitionism of Husserl's phenomenology with hermeneutics: every insight into what is possible is grasped and retained in a verbal formulation which calls for a sequel, another sentence that qualifies it, that builds on it, draws out a consequence, that evokes an objection to it, justifies it or supplies evidence for it. What marks authentic speech is not the adequacy of the insights it formulates but the commitment with which it is set forth to answer for all questions and all objections that can be put to it. It would then seem that authentic speech is formidably difficult: its words are those of common and generic language; its statements are open to indefinite confirmation.

Let us object that so much of what we report in our environment is really not open to an indefinite series of objections and doubts and its truth is not in suspense at the end of an unending series of verifications: it is plainly true and no real doubt arises about it. So much of what we would report in a foreign land the local people also would find to be plainly true. We can learn the names for these things in their language and can learn the ways their categories classify things where they are different from ours. Cf. Bernard Williams, *Truth and Truthfulness* (Princeton, N.J.: Princeton University Press, 2002), 45–53.

It is a mistake to make the reality and identity of what we see a hypothesis that only an unending series of explorations could fix and to make the reality of our perceived surroundings and the outlying world an always only probable hypothesis. Cf. Maurice Merleau-Ponty, *Phenomenology of Perception,* trans. Colin Smith (London: Routledge, 2000), xvi, 342–45; *The Visible and the Invisible,* trans. Alphonso Lingis (Evanston, Ill.: Northwestern University Press, 1968), 14–27.

Chapter 23

1. Kathleen Stewart, *A Space on the Side of the Road* (Princeton, N.J.: Princeton University Press, 1996).

Chapter 26

1. Ninety-four percent of university professors assessed themselves as better at their jobs than their average colleagues. Thomas Gilovich, *How We Know What Isn't So* (New York: Macmillan, 1991), 75–87.

2. Elster, *Sour Grapes,* 22.

3. David Hume, *A Treatise on Human Nature* (New York: Doubleday, 1961), 443.

Chapter 27

1. In *Torture: A Collection* (Oxford: Oxford University Press, 2004). Sanford Levinson, professor of government at the University of Texas at Austin; Jean Bethke Elshtain, University of Chicago political philosopher; Richard Posner, judge of the U.S. Court of Appeals and senior lecturer at the University of Chicago Law School; and Alan Dershowitz, Harvard University law professor—all work on ways to justify and institutionalize the torture which had become policy at Guantánamo and at Abu Ghraib and other secret prisons and was advocated by later Attorney General Alberto Gonzales.

Chapter 28

1. Ruth Benedict contended that for every character trait or impulse that is rejected as abnormal in our psychiatry, such as bellicose or suspicious character, anthropologists know of a well-documented culture in which it is positively valued. For example, trance, common and much studied in Bali, was common also in the European Middle Ages, where it had an established place in the discourse and practices of society; in the established discourse of contemporary Western culture, trance experiences are translated into the vocabulary of psychopathology as cases of character dissociation. However, it does seem that there is no culture that has been able to value all the drives and impulses in humans positively. Ruth Benedict, "Anthropology and the Abnormal," in *An Anthropologist at Work,* ed. Margaret Mead (Boston: Houghton Mifflin, 1959), 262–83.

Chapter 29

1. Daniel Paul Schreber, *Memoirs of My Nervous Illness,* trans. Ida Macalpine and Richard A. Hunter (London: W. Dawson, 1955).

2. Murders are judged by the state, which has arrogated to itself the exclusive use of violence, as assaults on society. Yet most murders, save those committed by cartels of organized crime or in gang wars, are "crimes of passion"—murders of the lover one has lost, one's rival, or even one's child or the child of a rival lover. Murders are committed by those who are seeking to regain lost honor or seeking to augment the few shreds of it that they still maintain. James Gilligan, a medical doctor who has worked extensively in prisons, explained:

> The purpose of violence is to diminish the intensity of shame and replace it as far as possible with its opposite, pride, thus preventing the individual from being overwhelmed by the feeling of shame. Violence toward others, such as homicide, is an attempt to replace shame with pride. . . . Behind the mask of "cool" or self-assurance that many violent men clamp onto their faces—with a desperation born of the certain knowledge that they would "lose face" if they ever let it slip—is a person who feels vulnerable not just to the "loss of face"

but to a total loss of honor, prestige, respect and status. (James Gilligan, *Violence: Our Deadly Epidemic and Its Causes* [New York: Putnam, 1996], 111–12)

3. The first Gulf War launched high-tech weaponry in which 250,000 people were killed, only 250 of them attacking soldiers, half of these by friendly fire; in the Kosovo war, no NATO troops were killed; in the 2001 assault on Afghanistan, one marine was killed. Wars are no longer fought on battlefields; the high-altitude aerial attacks are aimed to terrorize the civilian populations so that they reject their military leaders.

Photographs

Photographs by the author

About the Author

Alphonso Lingis is a professor emeritus of philosophy at Penn State University and the author of numerous books, including *The Imperative, Dangerous Emotions, Trust,* and, most recently, *Body Transformations.* He is also the preeminent English translator of Maurice Merleau-Ponty and Emmanuel Levinas. His translations include Merleau-Ponty's *The Visible and the Invisible* and Pierre Klossowski's *Sade My Neighbor,* both published by Northwestern University Press.